THE DEVELOPMENT
OF ARTHURIAN ROMANCE

The Development
of Arthurian Romance

ROGER SHERMAN LOOMIS

The Norton Library

W · W · NORTON & COMPANY · INC ·
NEW YORK

W. W. Norton & Company, Inc. is also the publisher of *The Norton Anthology of English Literature,* edited by M. H. Abrams, Robert M. Adams, David Daiches, E. Talbot Donaldson, George H. Ford, Samuel Holt Monk, and Hallett Smith; *The American Tradition in Literature,* edited by Sculley Bradley, Richmond Croom Beatty, and E. Hudson Long; *World Masterpieces,* edited by Maynard Mack, Kenneth Douglas, Howard E. Hugo, Bernard M. W. Knox, John C. McGalliard, P. M. Pasinetti, and René Wellek; *The Norton Reader,* edited by Arthur M. Eastman, Caesar R. Blake, Hubert M. English, Jr., Alan B. Howes, Robert T. Lenaghan, Leo F. McNamara, and James Rosier; and the NORTON CRITICAL EDITIONS, in hardcover and paperbound: authoritative texts, together with the leading critical interpretations, of major works of British, American, and Continental literature.

SBN 393-00518-6

PRINTED IN THE UNITED STATES OF AMERICA

1 2 3 4 5 6 7 8 9 0

CONTENTS

PREFACE

In this book I have endeavoured to write a history of Arthurian literature in the Middle Ages that will make intelligible a prodigious and puzzling phenomenon in the culture of Europe. If I have stressed origins and sources, it is because I believe with Vergil: *'Felix qui potuit rerum cognoscere causas.'* For, without understanding the forces which went to the making of a work of art, one cannot understand the work of art, and right understanding is the basis of all true appreciation. Needless to say, no one can pretend to analyse all the multiple and complex factors which entered into the composition of a masterpiece. Of course, there may be hidden influences and subliminal motives which only the author could reveal, and sometimes not even he. But medieval literature, far more than modern, is a product of tradition, and the Matter of Britain, even more than other medieval narrative genres, requires a knowledge of mingling racial and cultural streams.

Hence the modern scholar and critic has advantages over the medieval reader of Arthurian romance and in some respects over the romancer himself. In our libraries we have the means of detecting many things about his material which he could never have known or even suspected. By comparison with other texts we can sometimes assess what share of credit should go to him and what share should go to his predecessors. We can avoid some of the baseless and wild theorizing founded on ignorance of the man, his times, and the tradition which he inherited.

Some critics have complained that a study of sources and origins is 'a flight from the masterpiece', and it is true that many scholars of the past tended to ignore the purely literary techniques and values of the works which they edited and

7

studied, devoting all their attention to linguistic, textual, and historic matters. But it may be said in partial justification that many a medieval romance is artless to the point where a discussion of its art would be much ado about nothing. Bardolatry today sometimes takes the form of discerning structural patterns, symbolic meanings, and profound concepts where hitherto readers have been content to see no more than a straightforward tale of love and adventure. Yet the same narrative may be of great historical interest, offer fascinating insights into the development of a theme, and provide a solution to the mysteries of a masterpiece. Some critics, indeed, who seem to advocate a complete neglect of literary history, of source study, and of the author and his milieu, who imply that all one needs is to read a text in order to understand and evaluate it, do in practice make careful comparisons with its immediate sources and draw conclusions. They are not so extreme as their pronouncements would lead one to believe. They do not recommend the study of a work of art in a vacuum. There is actually a considerable measure of agreement between the 'new critics' and the objects of their attack.

They are right, of course, in asserting that the question of who Arthur was, and when and where he flourished, has nothing to do with the understanding and appreciation of Chrétien de Troyes's poems, where he is not even distinguished as a fighting man, but is, on the contrary, belittled. But is the question of no importance? After all, if there had been no Arthur, and if he had not endeared himself to his people, there would have been no Arthurian romance, no Chrétien de Troyes, no Malory. It matters not at all that there were Pictish kings named Drust or Drustan, but is it of small interest that to one of them there was attached as early as the ninth century a legend which is reflected in the combat of Tristan with Morolt and his recognition in the bath by the Princess Isolt? The fact that we find Arthur associated in obscure early poems with Welsh and Irish divinities might seem of concern merely to antiquarians, but it is the presence of these mythical figures which helps us to account for and interpret the solar traits of Gawain, the inconsistencies of Morgan le Fay, the monstrous features of the Grail Messenger, and, indeed, most of the supernatural machinery peculiar to the Matter of Britain. On the other hand, the discovery in a twelfth-century Persian text of a very close parallel to the famous scene in which Sir Bedivere cast Excalibur into the mere warns us that not all the marvels of Britain are derived from the Celts.

The careful and thorough investigation of sources and analogues has, therefore, not only a positive value but also a negative one, almost equally important. It may and should save us from wild theorizing about the content and the intent of an episode or a work. There are many traps for the eager and the unwary, and I have fallen into them myself. It has been proposed that the Green Knight is the principle of vegetation incarnate, that he is akin to the Green Man of English Mayday games, and that he was taken over directly from heathenish rites observed by the medieval poet. A very alluring theory, until one recalls, first, that the author of *Gawain and the Green Knight* was in all probability the author of three of the most devoutly religious poems in the language, and would have been horrified by the accusation that he had represented sympathetically a custom reeking of paganism; and, secondly, that the strongest evidence points to the origin of the Beheading Test in an Irish saga where the counterpart of the Green Knight has no vegetable or arboreal features. Nor are there any such features in the Green Knight's other self, the hospitable huntsman. In both the Irish saga and the Welsh *mabinogi*, in which the hospitable huntsman appears, there are clear traces of myth, but not of ritual. And the same may be said of that other medley of motifs, the Grail legend. Such rites as are connected with the Grail are Christian and have been introduced as a result of Christian misinterpretation of pagan myths.

The reaction against the study of sources has led to the discovery in medieval literature of meanings and intentions which we may feel sure were never realized by the author. Professor C. S. Lewis has been impressed by this phenomenon in the case of his own fictions:

> Some published fantasies of my own have had foisted on them (often by the kindliest critics) so many admirable allegorical meanings that I never dreamed of as to throw me into doubt whether it is possible for the wit of man to devise anything in which the wit of some other man cannot find, and plausibly find, an allegory.

It may be an amusing parlour game to see how far one can go in interpreting the Nun's Priest's Tale as an allegory in which the hen-wife represents Ecclesia, the fox Diabolus, and Chauntecleer Humanum Genus. Chaucer himself might have enjoyed the game, but since he gave no hint of such an *interpretatio christiana* of a beast epic, we may feel sure that it had not occurred to him. If Chaucer thought of his gallinaceous hero at all as a type, it would probably be in the terms of a brilliant critic and scholar: 'Chauntecleer is mankind trying to adjust the universe to his own specifications and failing—though not, I believe, fatally.' But the poet's *principal* aim was surely less cosmic and more comic—to extract all the fun he could out of the behaviour and fate of Chauntecleer by endowing him and his harem with incongruous human attributes and by tricking out a barnyard comedy with mock heroics, pompous rhetoric, and moral solemnity. Are not the maxims with which the tale ends a part of the jest?

It may be taken for granted, I believe, that when a medieval author intended his readers to see allegorical or symbolic meanings, he made them quite plain. In his day, as in ours, there was no consistent science of significations. To us, green may stand for the Emerald Isle, ignorance, jealousy, and 'go ahead!' For our ancestors a peacock could be interpreted in sixteen different ways. Therefore, the poet of *Gawain and the Green Knight* was at pains to expound in detail the significances he attached to the pentangle, the five-pointed star on Gawain's shield; and Malory, following the French *Quest of the Holy Grail*, explicates the typology and symbolism of King Solomon's Ship and the Sword of Strange Hangings. It is a safe corollary to draw concerning the great bulk of medieval narrative that the author, far from trying to obscure his meaning, as some scholars would have us believe, endeavoured to make it clear. Sometimes, of course, he did not wholly succeed; sometimes he was himself vague or confused; sometimes in writing for his contemporaries he introduced topics and used expressions which require anno-tation or commentary. In the *Divine Comedy*, needless to say, there is much that does not lie on the surface, but that work is in an entirely different category from the romances of chivalry.[1] To invest these with occult significances and arcane symbolisms is to mistake the nature of the genre and of the audiences to which it appealed.

What is, in my opinion, the most fantastic aberration in recent studies of medieval literature is the assumption that Freud and Jung with their still hypothetical theories about the unconscious are the best interpreters of authors about whose conscious aims we know a great deal. Artistic procedures and techniques which are appropriately and rightly ascribed to James Joyce and Dylan Thomas are anachronistically credited to comparatively unsophisticated authors of five hundred or more years ago. To inject twentieth-century ideologies and fashions into the literatures of the twelfth and thirteenth centuries is as naive as the notorious exegesis of the Song of Solomon as prefiguring the love of Christ for the Church, and more naive than the tongue-in-cheek treatment of Ovid's *Metamorphoses* as pious parables.

My task, as I have conceived it, then, has been to interpret within limitations of space a significant and perplexing body of literature, not with tools adapted to the elucidation of works of our own day, not with the aid of historically

[1] See *Critical Approaches to Medieval Literature*, ed. Dorothy Bethurum (New York, 1960), pp. 1–26, 61–82.

unrelated cults and cultures, but as originated and shaped by historic events, and by intellectual and artistic forces which demonstrably affected the peoples and persons who contributed to the Matter of Britain. As for underlying *sententiae*, I recognize only those which the authors themselves expressed or clearly implied. Mistakes I have made, of course; important matters have been neglected or ignored for obvious reasons; much remains obscure. But of the historical approach and the historical method I have no doubt.

ROGER SHERMAN LOOMIS

ARTHURIAN ORIGINS

ONE of the great riddles of literary history is: whence, why, and how did the great mass of fiction centred about Arthur arise and become the favourite reading of lords and ladies, young and old, not only in England and France, but also in Italy, Spain, and Germany? Even as early as 1170 the spread of Arthur's renown caused a certain Alanus to exclaim: 'Whither has not flying fame spread and familiarized the name of Arthur the Briton, even as far as the empire of Christendom extends? Who does not speak of Arthur the Briton, since he is almost better known to the peoples of Asia Minor than to the *Britanni* [the Welsh and Cornish]?' Apparently, reports of Arthur's prowess had been carried by the Crusaders to the Near East. The greatest of medieval authors were captivated by the bizarre adventures of the knights of the Round Table. In the thirteenth century Wolfram von Eschenbach composed his masterpiece, *Parzival*, the main inspiration of Wagner's opera. In the next century Dante expressed his admiration for the most beautiful mazes of Arthurian story. Only with the Renaissance and the Reformation did these centuries-old tales of quest and conquest, of fairy loves and fatal passion, 'of tourneys and of trophies hung, of forests and enchantments drear, where more is meant than meets the ear', go out of fashion. But not without leaving many permanent effects on life and literature. The word 'romance' itself owes its main connotations to the romances of the Round Table—strange adventure and idealistic love.

Anyone endowed with a modicum of curiosity who considers this fact and who reads widely in the literature concerned with Arthur, Guenevere, Merlin, Vivien, Lancelot, Tristram, and Galahad, will come to realize that here is not one problem that calls for solution, but many problems. If in childhood you were fascinated by the wild tales of the Welsh *Mabinogion*, were later introduced to the *Idylls of the King*, and still later have listened enthralled to Wagner's operas of *Tristan and Isolde* and *Parsifal*, you must have asked yourself whence these legends came, whether there was in them any kernel of historic fact, how they came to be recorded in Welsh, English, and German, and why there are such amazing inconsistencies, even in the same poem or book, as to the characters and their careers.

If, in bewilderment, you have sought information from authoritative sources, you may have found no general agreement among them as to the historicity of Arthur; the contribution of the Irish and the Welsh to the French romances and their derivatives; the presence or absence of Celtic myths in the stories of Tristan, Morgan le Fay, and Gawain; the amount of influence which that fraudulent chronicle, the *History of the Kings of Britain* by Geoffrey of Monmouth, exerted on the early romances. As for the origin and meaning of the Grail legend, one may take one's pick at of least a score of rival theories, supported by much erudition. In recent years we have been offered arcane symbolisms and structural subtleties as affording the true explanations of the eccentricities of Arthurian romance, and there is no author whose character, originality, and intentions are not the subjects of debate.

Of course, this situation is not unique and not confined to medieval literature. Who has not heard of the Homeric question, the Baconian, the Marlovian, and the Oxfordian theories of the identity of Shakespeare, and the multiple interpretations of Melville's *Moby Dick*. But the Arthurian problems are more difficult to solve since they take us into very remote times, places, cultures, and literatures with which few of us are familiar; and the evidence is not only strange but also complex. Practical-minded persons and aesthetically sensitive critics may well demand whether it is worth while to follow up studies so exotic and intricate in order to attain results so uncertain. Is it not enough to read the *Mabinogion* or Malory's prose epic or Gottfried von Strassburg's *Tristan* or Tennyson's *Idylls* or T. H. White's *The Once and Future King* for pure enjoyment? Is not the search for origins and influences really a 'flight from the master-piece'?

Now the *raison d'être* of any work of art lies in the responses of those who see, hear, or read it, but its value lies only in the responses of those who are attuned to it; and in the realm of literature that means those who understand it. In its fullest sense, understanding means knowing its creator, the materials he worked with, what he did with them, and why. When one cannot know the author, one must be content with some knowledge of his milieu and his age. The reader who is content with his subjective reactions alone runs the risk of interpreting the work of art in a fashion which would evoke peals of laughter from the author. He also shows his lack of interest in the creative process which produced the work of art.

This book assumes an interest in the vast and complicated process which produced a literature that fascinated and still fascinates its readers, even in spite of crudities and obscurities. This book will attempt to cover the history of that literature from its beginnings down to 1500 in such a way as to make it understandable, and, in the case of the major works, to that extent more enjoyable. After all, in spite of clashing theories, there has accumulated in the past hundred years enough evidence to settle most of the crucial questions relating to the origin and development of the Arthurian cycle, the Matter of Britain as it has been called. Many minor mysteries will remain. Where precisely did Arthur inflict those defeats on the Saxon invaders which made him the idol and the hope of the Welsh for over a thousand years? How much of fact and how much of 'frame-up' was in the criminal indictments against Sir Thomas Malory? What were the dates of the early French romances? How would Chrétien de Troyes have ended his poem on the Grail if he had lived to complete it? The history which I will sketch and the interpretations I will offer will not go undisputed, but they are the result of a lifetime of study and reflection and a conscientious attempt to weigh the evidence for rival theories. And now for a consideration of Arthur himself and the earliest forms of his story.

Was King Arthur a man or a myth? That is the question on everyone's tongue as soon as the name is mentioned. If it had been put to a panel of experts two generations ago, the majority would probably have pronounced in favour of myth. But they would not have agreed as to whether he was a battle-god, a bear-god, a 'culture-hero', a Celtic Zeus, or a deity presiding over agriculture. Today, if the same question were put to a similar panel, there would be a strong majority who would agree that he was a man. But there would still be violent disagreement as to whether the narratives which grew up about him and the knights of the Round Table contained a considerable element of Celtic mythology.

We know the names of quite a few divinities worshipped in the British Isles, some recorded in inscriptions, some in the *Mabinogion*, but there is not one god who bears a name resembling Arthur's. On the other hand, the experts agree that the Roman name Artorius was not unknown in Britain and that it would have developed normally into the Welsh form Arthur, just as Constantinus became Custennin. Arthur, then, was human, not divine. What kind of man was he? The earliest reference which suggests the answer to this question is found in a Welsh poem, the *Gododdin*, most of which goes back to the seventh century or earlier. It is a lament for the British warriors who fell in battle with the Angles somewhere in northern England. Of one warrior it is said that 'he glutted black ravens on the rampart of the fort, though he was not Arthur'. In other words, he did not feed the corbies with as many carcasses as did Arthur, the nonpareil.

The *locus classicus* for the historic Arthur and his activities is a passage in the *Historia Britonum*, composed by Nennius, a priest of South Wales, about 800. There we read that after the death of Hengist (*c.*488), the Jutish conqueror of Kent, his son Octa came down from the north, and that Arthur fought against him, together with the kings of the Britons, but he himself was the battle-leader—in modern parlance, the commander-in-chief. There follows a list of twelve victories, and their sites are named. The eighth took place at *castellum Guinnion*, 'when Arthur bore the image of the holy Virgin Mary on his shoulders [probably a mistranslation of the Welsh word for shield], and when the pagans were put to flight and a great slaughter made of them through the might of our Lord Jesus Christ and of Holy Mary his mother'. The twelfth battle was on Mount Badon, where there fell nine hundred and sixty men before Arthur's single onset. Though one detects in this account error and gross exaggeration, there is certainly corroboration of his physical prowess; and his Christianity, though probably genuine enough, was of the muscular variety. The list of battle sites does not seem to be reliable, for though two of them can be identified with certainty—Coet Celidon and the City of the Legion, namely, the forest region of Strathclyde and Chester—it is most unlikely that there were, at the time indicated, any Germanic invaders for Arthur to fight so far to the north and west. There can be no doubt, however, that the battle of Mount Badon was a great victory of the Britons, for the British St Gildas, writing about 540, assures us that as a result the Saxon conquest of southern England was checked, and forty-four years of peace followed. Though Gildas does not mention Arthur, it is hard to refuse credit to the renowned battle-leader for this memorable triumph. The date may safely be set about the year 500, and though Mount Badon has not been identified, it must lie in the pathway of the Saxon conquest, west of Kent and east of the Salisbury plain.

We have only to realize what the situation of the Britons was at the end of the fifth century in order to understand why the victor of Mount Badon was enshrined in the memory of their descendants for a thousand years as the incomparable hero of their race. Gildas gives us a lurid picture.

> The columns [of the churches] were levelled with the ground by the frequent strokes of the battering-ram, all the farmers routed, together with their bishops, priests, and people, whilst the sword gleamed, and the flames crackled round them on every side . . . In the midst of the streets lay the tops of lofty towers, tumbled to the ground, stones of high walls, holy altars, fragments of human bodies, covered with livid clots of coagulated blood, looking as if they had been squeezed together in a press, and with no chance of being buried, save in the ruins of houses or in the ravening bellies of wild beasts and birds.

From this fate, as if by a miracle, Arthur delivered his country-men for a time. Three hundred and seventy-five years later Alfred delivered the English from the heathen Danes, and so became 'England's darling'. By the victory of Mount Badon, it seems, Arthur became the Messiah of the Britons, destined to return one day as their Saviour even after they had been driven down into Cornwall or across the Channel to Brittany. For the peace came to an end; the Saxon drive westward was resumed; in 552 the Britons were defeated at Old Sarum and were relentlessly pushed back to the line of the Severn. But the memory of that bright period when Arthur had given them security and confidence once more still glowed in their hearts.

The *Annals of Wales*, compiled about 950, contain two entries relating to Arthur. The first assigns the victory of Badon to the year 516, and the second records under the year 537 the battle of Camlann, at which Arthur and Medraut fell. These datings have been questioned and may be ten or fifteen years off either way. The second makes it certain that Modred was a historical person, and it is probable that, in accordance with later literary tradition, he and Arthur were opposed in battle. But we are not told that he was Arthur's nephew and a treacherous villain, nor does anyone know where Camlann is. What we can be sure of is that about this battle developed what many consider the most majestic scenes of all Arthurian romance.

From Gildas, Nennius, and the *Annals of Wales*, which give us what little we know about the historic Arthur, let us turn to the early Welsh fragments of a non-historic tradition. In them he appears as a redoubtable warrior, but he is not yet a king, and, strange to say, there is not a word of the Saxons. Included in Nennius's *Historia Britonum* there is a list of *mirabilia*, wonderful phenomena, and among them are two connected with *Arthurus miles*. Near Builth was a cairn, and on top of it was a remarkable stone which had been marked with the footprint of Arthur's hound Cabal during the hunting of the boar named Troit. The boar and the hound reappear, as we shall see, in the Welsh tale of *Kulhwch and Olwen*, and the name Carn Cavall, the Cairn of Cabal, still clings to a hill in the region. A second marvel Nennius claims to have observed himself—the grave or tomb of Arthur's son Amr, which, when measured, varied in length from six to fifteen feet. This elastic grave is no longer to be seen, but the site can be visited, for a spring near by, called Licat Amr, has been identified with the source of the River Gamber in Herefordshire.

Far more significant than these local legends for the light they shed on the development of Arthurian romance are two Welsh poems of the tenth or the eleventh century. The first is a fragmentary dialogue between Arthur and a gate-warden, who demands that Arthur name his companions. Arthur complies and also tells the exploits of some of them. We easily recognize Kay (Kei) and Bedivere (Beduir), though it is startling to find that the often discomfited seneschal of the later romances is here exalted above all the rest of Arthur's retinue as a destroyer of lions and witches, and as more than a match for a demon cat, Cath Paluc, doubtless the Chapalu whom Arthur is credited with overcoming in a French romance of *Merlin*. Highly significant is the presence among Arthur's warriors of three Celtic deities. Mabon is Apollo Maponos, worshipped in pre-Christian Britain. Manawidan son of Llyr is the Welsh counterpart of the Irish sea-god Manannan son of Ler. Lluch Llauynnauc, there is good reason to believe, was similarly derived from the Irish god of sun and storm, Lugh or Luch Lamhfada.

Here, then, there has been a startling evolution. Arthur is not yet elevated to the rank of king, but he is associating with gods, not as an equal, but as a superior. It is not difficult to see what this implies. Though Britain, under Roman domination, had been partly Christianized in the second century, the Welsh in the tenth century still remembered the heathen divinities as beings, endowed with supernatural powers, who had lived long ago. The clergy might condemn them as devils, but the laity were more tolerant. To be sure, the reputation of these gods and goddesses was variable, but, roughly speaking, they seem to have played in the imagination of the Welsh a part not unlike that of the deities in Homer. In the oldest literature of Wales there is a mingling of the divine with the human and real which reminds one of the *Iliad* and the *Odyssey*.

Another most noteworthy fact is that, though Mabon was in origin a god of the Britons, Manawidan son of Llyr and Lluch Llauynnauc were imported from Ireland. Far from being exceptional, this absorption of Irish mythic and heroic lore into Welsh literature was entirely normal, and it has been proved that certain stories in the Welsh *Mabinogion* can be understood only by comparison with Irish analogues. Accordingly, when in due course we shall discern in the fabric of French and English fictions of the Arthurian cycle Irish narrative patterns blended with Welsh, there is no cause for surprise or scepticism. It is no wonder that the career of the Irish god Lugh Lamhfada corresponds on eight points to that of Lancelot du Lac.

Whereas the dialogue between Arthur and the gate-warden introduces us to the Celtic gods, the second archaic poem, entitled the *Spoils of Annwn*, gives us a composite picture of their abode. The first translator found the text so obscure that

he exclaimed: 'Could Lycophron or the Sybils, or any ancient
oracle, be more elaborately incomprehensible?' Even contemporaries of the poet must have found it something of a puzzle,
for, like much modern poetry, it was full of allusions which
could be recognized only by the cognoscenti, those familiar
with traditional lore. But most of the obscurity is dissipated
once it is understood that the word Annwn (pronounced
Ánoon) does not mean Hades, though often so translated, but
the dwelling-place of the pagan gods; and that the main
theme of the poem is a raid by Arthur and his men on this
island elysium to carry off as plunder the cauldron of its lord,
the Head of Annwn. The vessel, tended by nine maidens,
had the property of testing the mettle of warriors, for it
would not boil meat for a coward. Annwn is referred to under
other names—Fairy Fortress, Fortress of Revelry, Four-
cornered Fortress, Fortress of Glass; and these names and
certain descriptive details found in the poem make us realize
how various were the conceptions which prevailed about this
home of the old divinities. Certain lines imply that it was an
island of the sea; others that it was a dimly lit, subterranean
region. At the cost of many lives was the cauldron obtained,
for only seven returned from the expedition, including, of
course, Arthur and the same Lluch whom he mentions in his
dialogue with the gate-warden.

If one is interested solely or mainly in the classics of
Arthurian romance, such as the poems of Chrétien de Troyes,
the *Parzival*, and *Sir Gawain and the Green Knight*, or in the
modern masterpieces, one may well ask whether these early
puzzle-poems have any relevance, and the answer may seem
to be 'No'. One looks in vain in later literature for the cauldron,
or the nine maidens who tended it. But one does find in the
romances three testing vessels—the Grail, a horn, a cup—and
the nine sorceresses of the Shining Fortress (Caer Loyw).
The island elysium of the Welsh poem reappears, much
sanctified, in the thirteenth-century French romance of
Perlesvaus, as the final destination of the hero.

We can safely conclude, therefore, that the Matter of

Britain originated in the blending of historic reminiscences of a British battle-leader with a highly fanciful mythological tradition going back to pagan times. It is in the *Historia Britonum* of the Welsh priest Nennius and in the Welsh poetry of the Dark Ages that we see this strange hybrid plant sending down its roots into the rich soil of pagan Britain and putting out the buds which were destined to flower so luxuriantly in the romances of the Round Table.

2

THE *MABINOGION*

In 1849 Lady Charlotte Guest, the literary wife of a steel magnate, completed the publication of twelve Welsh tales in prose, together with a translation which became a minor English classic and inspired two of Tennyson's *Idylls of the King*, as well as Peacock's rollicking burlesque, the *Misfortunes of Elphin*. The title which Lady Guest gave to the collection, the *Mabinogion* (pronounced Mabinóg-yon), does not mean, as she supposed, 'tales for children', but 'tales of a hero's birth, infancy, and youth'. There is, however, a wide variety in the nature of the narratives, and only three conform to the correct definition. To complicate matters still further, the first four tales are called the Four Branches of the Mabinogi, though only one of these, relating the birth and boyhood of Gwri of the Golden Hair, seems to deserve the title.

The Four Branches were probably composed by a single author about 1060, and represent a blending of various strands of Celtic myth which had, to begin with, little or no connection with each other. Matthew Arnold recognized in his *Lectures on Celtic Literature* both the charm and the true nature of the material: 'Who is the mystic Arawn, the king of Annwn, who changed semblance for a year with Pwyll, prince of Dyved, and reigned in his place? These are no medieval personages; they belong to an older mythological world.' And again: 'The very first thing that strikes one in reading the *Mabinogion* is how evidently the medieval story-teller is pillaging an antiquity of which he does not fully possess the secret; he is like a peasant building his house on the site of Halicarnassus or Ephesus.' The researches of the

23

last hundred years have fully confirmed Arnold's impression and have demonstrated that in the Four Branches, along with myths of British origin, there are similar elements directly borrowed from Ireland.

Very few scholars have realized the great importance of the Four Branches of the Mabinogi for the study of Arthurian romance. Since Arthur himself is absent and none of the prominent knights and ladies of his court is easily recognizable, the tales until lately have been generally ignored. But take the very first episode—the compact of friendship between Arawn, the supernatural huntsman, and Pwyll; Pwyll's lying with Arawn's wife in Arawn's shape; his fidelity and chastity under temptation. While, on the one hand, there is a clear affinity to the Irish story of Manannan and Fiachna's wife, there is an even more remarkable relationship to the experiences of Gawain at the Green Knight's castle in the English poetic masterpiece. Not that this Welsh text of the eleventh century was the literary source, even at several removes, of the four-teenth-century English poem; but both were indebted, apparently, to a well-known Welsh tradition of the temptation of a hero by the wife of the huntsman king, Arawn. In other supernatural figures of the Four Branches, we have the proto-types of the enchantress Vivien, who beguiled Merlin, and of the Maimed King of the Grail romances, Wagner's Amfortas. Originally, of course, these mythical personages had no relationship to the tales circulating about Arthur, but by the twelfth century they had been attracted into his orbit.

The earliest surviving story in which the heroic Arthur is surrounded by figures drawn from this primitive world and by others assembled from folklore and history is included in the *Mabinogion* under the title *Kulhwch and Olwen*. Probably copied down about 1100, it might be called a *mabinogi* (though it is not one of the Four Branches), for it recounts the fortunes of a prince from birth to marriage, and frequently refers to him as a *mab*; that is, a boy or youth. On the other hand, it fore-shadows distinctly the typical romance of two centuries later: the hero is a near kinsman of Arthur; love is the impelling force; quests form the staple of his adventures; and his reward is the hand of a beautiful bride. Arthur, at last elevated to the rank of 'sovereign prince of this island', presides over a host of warriors, and when Kulhwch names them we are not surprised to meet again our previous acquaintances: Kei, Bedwir, Lluch (spelled Llwch), Mabon son of Modron, and Manawidan son of Llyr.

Kulhwch and Olwen differs markedly from the Four Branches in the comparative paucity of strictly mythological elements. The main plot is known to folklorists as the 'Giant's Daughter', and it is not hard to discern a likeness in outline to a famous example of the type: the Greek romance of Jason, Medea, and the Golden Fleece. Prince Kulhwch is put under a taboo by his stepmother never to marry anyone except Olwen, daughter of the Giant Ysbaddaden. Filled with longing, although he has never seen her, he seeks the help of Arthur and all his host, naming each one. Never was a more heterogeneous company. Together with those already mentioned there were Gildas the saint, Taliesin the bard, and several 'helpful companions', like those who joined the Argonauts. There was Ear son of Hearer, who though buried seven fathoms below ground could hear an ant rising in the morning fifty miles away. There was the Tracker, who could track down the swine which had been carried off seven years before he was born. Accompanied by a troop of Arthur's men, Kulhwch entered Ysbaddaden's hall. 'Where are those rascal servants and those ruffians of mine?' said the giant. 'Raise up the forks under my eyelids that I may see my future son-in-law.' But only after Kulhwch has flung a poisoned spear through his eyeball will Ysbaddaden state the conditions under which he will consent to Kulhwch's becoming his son-in-law; namely, thirty-nine tasks which must be performed in order to provide a suitable wedding feast and to enable Ysbaddaden to appear properly shaved and groomed for the occasion. With the aid of Arthur and his men, Kulhwch carries out the tasks, one by one, and obtains scissors, a comb, and a razor from between the ears of the savage boar, Twrch Trwyth. He then presents himself before the giant; Cadw of Pictland shaves him, cutting off at the same time the flesh and the ears, and Goreu chops off his head. 'That night Kulhwch slept with Olwen, and she was his only wife.' Thus ends this curious medley of the grotesque, the gruesome, and the romantic.

Fitted into the main plot of the 'Giant's Daughter' are many traditional stories. We have already met Twrch Trwyth as the boar Troit in Nennius's list of *mirabilia*; and Arthur's hunting of the beast from its lair in Ireland, across St George's Channel, over a devious course through South Wales, and down into Cornwall is represented as one of the most perilous of the tasks assigned to Kulhwch, and it is treated with extraordinary geographical precision. Similarly, the raid of Arthur on Annwn to procure a magic cauldron, which was the subject of the cryptic poem treated in the first chapter, is converted into another of the tasks imposed by Ysbaddaden. Here the strange glamour has been dispelled, and we have only a prosaic account of an attack on the King of Ireland's steward to obtain a cauldron to boil meat for Kulhwch's wedding banquet.

But the general impression is one of ebullient vigour and wide-ranging fancy. And there are passages of poetic charm such as the description of Olwen, whose hair was yellower than the flower of the broom, whose skin whiter than the foam of the wave, and whose eye was fairer than that of the thrice-mewed falcon. And look at Kulhwch as he canters off to Arthur's court. 'A gold-hilted sword was at his thigh, the blade of which was of gold, and he carried a gold-chased buckler with the colour of heaven's lightning in it, and the boss was of ivory. Before him were two brindled, white-breasted greyhounds, having strong collars of rubies about their necks, reaching from the shoulder to the ear. The one that was on the left side bounded across to the right side, and the one on the right to the left, and like two sea-swallows sported around him.'

Although the tale of Kulhwch could not have been read outside Wales, Cornwall, and Brittany, and was not the source of any French romance, one should not overlook the fact that Chrétien de Troyes, who wrote the first French Arthurian romances, used two of the situations already employed by his Welsh predecessor. One has only to read the account of Kulhwch's arrival and reception at Arthur's court, and then turn to Chrétien's story of Perceval's arrival and reception at the same court, in order to perceive that here is no accidental resemblance, that here we have two versions of the same Welsh tradition. Likewise the dialogue between Kulhwch and a herdsman has its counterpart in Chrétien's *Ivain*.

The most sophisticated effort in Lady Guest's collection is the *Dream of Rhonabwy*. Composed at least a hundred years later than *Kulhwch*, it was designed to create the phantasmagoric effect of a dream, and also to serve as a memory test for a reciter, as the last sentence proclaims: 'No one, neither bard nor story-teller, knows the *Dream* without a book because of the number of colours that were on the horses and all the different kinds of rare colours both on the arms and the panoply, and on the precious mantles and the magic stones.'

The opening scene offers a deliberate contrast to this opulence and splendour. One stormy night Rhonabwy, a man of Powys, took refuge in a filthy, smoky cow-barn and went to sleep on an ox-hide. He dreamed that he was riding with two companions towards a ford of the Severn where it passed from Wales into England, and was pursued and overtaken by a youth clad in green and yellow and mounted on a green-and-yellow horse. Rhonabwy learned that his pursuer had deliberately provoked the battle of Camlann, in which, as we remember, Arthur and Medraut (Modred) fell. But, with a dreamlike indifference to chronology, when Rhonabwy reached the ford, he saw Arthur still alive, apparently of huge size, seated on an island in the river, attended by a bishop and a white-skinned youth costumed in black. Arthur smiled grimly when Rhonabwy and his companions approached, because such 'little fellows' as these were now the defenders of Britain. Troop after troop of horsemen, each troop uniformly garbed in a single colour, rode up, and we learn with astonishment that they were mustering for the battle of Badon, to take place at midday.

The army now set out along the valley of the Severn, and was joined by a Scandinavian troop led by King Mark and a Danish troop under Edern. Before the walls of Caer Baddon, here equated with Bath, the host dismounted. Kai came dashing into the midst, he and his horse clad in mail as white as the water-lily, with rivets as red as blood.

There follows a scene of dreamlike irrelevance. Arthur started playing a game with Owain (Malory's Uwaine) son of Urien on a board of silver with gold pieces. Messengers, each minutely described, arrived one after another to complain that Arthur's squires were wounding and killing Owain's ravens, and though Owain protested Arthur refused each time to restrain the squires. At last, in a fury, Owain commanded that his standard be raised, whereupon the ravens recovered their magical powers, swooped on the squires, and tore them to pieces. It was now Arthur's turn to beg Owain to intervene, but in vain. Only when Arthur crushed the golden pieces on the board did Owain cause his standard to be lowered and peace returned.

The impending battle of Baddon did not take place, for Arthur's prospective foe, Osla, the Octa of Nennius, sent horsemen to ask for a truce. A council was held, the truce was agreed to, Kai rose to urge all who chose to follow Arthur to be with him that night in Cornwall. With the consequent commotion Rhonabwy awoke.

This narrative anticipates in curious ways a nightmare described by De Quincey, though there is not here the sense of terror and helplessness which the Opium Eater conveys: 'the feeling of a vast march—of infinite cavalcades filing off . . . The morning was come of a mighty day. . . . Somewhere, I knew not where—somehow, I knew not how—by some beings, I knew not whom—a battle, a strife, an agony, was conducting—was evolving like a great drama or piece of music.' The Welsh author prefers a lighter mood, and the conclusion is deliberate anticlimax, but there can be little doubt of his success in reproducing the incoherence of our nocturnal adventures by the use of anachronism, the introduction of unexpected characters, rapid shifts of place, and particularly by the insertion of so irrelevant a theme as the chess-game and the concomitant battle of the ravens—who, investigation has shown, were the bird-forms of Owain's goddess-mother Modron and her companions, eerie survivors from British heathendom. But along with this archaic element we may detect comparatively late touches: the influence of Geoffrey of Monmouth's mendacious chronicle probably accounts for the identification of Baddon with Bath, and for the concept of Arthur as an emperor to whom the men of Scandinavia and Denmark owed allegiance and to whom the Isles of Greece paid tribute.

Quite different in character from *Kulhwch* and the *Dream of Rhonabwy* is a group of three Arthurian romances, *Geraint*, the *Lady of the Fountain*, and *Peredur*. In each the sequence of incidents corresponds more or less closely to that in one of three poems by Chrétien de Troyes, who wrote in the latter half of the twelfth century; in each, mythological and primitive elements are much less conspicuous; and the geography of the *Lady of the Fountain* and *Peredur* evinces none of that precise knowledge of Wales and its borders as do the two tales previously discussed. There has been a long and heated controversy about whether their resemblance to Chrétien's famous romances is due to rather hazy and inaccurate reminiscences or to the indebtedness of both to a common French or Anglo-Norman source. On grounds of antecedent probability one might guess that the Welsh tales are re-tellings of Chrétien's celebrated stories. But a detailed examination of the resemblances and differences does not support this conjecture. *Geraint* and the *Lady of the Fountain* seem rather to be based on the lost work of a single author who wrote in French about the middle of the twelfth century two extraordinarily realistic and cleverly constructed novelettes dealing with love and marriage. Geraint, as readers of Tennyson's

Idylls will remember, won his beautiful bride Enid by his victory over the Knight of the Sparrowhawk, was moved by a false suspicion of her fidelity to put her through a series of severe tests, and at the same time demonstrated his prowess anew; and so, his faith in her and her pride in him restored, they lived happily thereafter. The *Lady of the Fountain* is cast in a similar mould. Owain son of Urien won his beautiful bride by his victory over the Knight of the Fountain, but, after a brief honeymoon, lost her love by his absorption in knightly sports. Only after a period of estrangement did he win his lady's forgiveness by his prowess, and live with her thereafter at Arthur's court till the end of her days. Though in each of these romances there are still supernatural features —the dwarf king in one, the storm-making spring in the other —the natural motivation and the concern with practical problems of conduct show that the unknown author lived in a very different world from that inhabited by the author of *Kulhwch*. It should not be forgotten that *Geraint* and the *Lady of the Fountain* are not translations from a written text but rather re-tellings based on memory, and the conclusions especially have suffered as a result.

Peredur had somewhat the same history in that it was spun out of defective memories of French or Anglo-Norman tales of Perceval. One of these sources may have been Chrétien's poem about the hero, but, if so, it has been catastrophically disarranged and expanded. For example, the hero, who is more familiar to us as the virgin knight of Malory's book and of Wagner's *Parsifal*, is represented as pledging his love to three ladies in succession and with the third he lived for fourteen years. Did the author intend to depict Peredur as a reformed Don Juan? More probably he merely stitched together, haphazard, three independent love-stories which had grown up about the hero. Though he introduced a scene corresponding clearly to Perceval's visit to the Grail castle, he placed in the vessel corresponding to the Grail a man's severed head, swimming in blood. When we learn later that the head was that of Peredur's cousin and that Peredur was

under an obligation to avenge him, the confusion is even
more patent still. This Welsh text, judged as art, stands at
the very nadir, but as a literary detective puzzle it stands
very high.

The *Mabinogion*, then, consists of four different strata in
the development of Arthurian fiction: 1, the Four Branches,
made up largely of mythical material, Welsh and Irish, as yet
unattached to Arthur; 2, *Kulhwch*, in which we find a slight
amount of this same material, together with a preponderance
of widespread folktale motifs, the whole being attracted into
the orbit of Arthur; 3, the *Dream of Rhonabwy*, a highly successful experiment in combining very archaic traditions about
Arthur and Owain with recent pseudo-historical additions,
to give the vivid impression of a dream; 4, three romances
which, though incorporating much material of ultimate
Welsh and Irish origin, have their immediate sources in
French or Anglo-Norman compositions of the twelfth century.
Still the continuity of the tradition may be discerned sometimes dimly, sometimes clearly, in its variegated manifestations. And Arthur, who had vanished from this earthly
scene in the early sixth century, an obscure figure, remembered
only by his fellow Britons, has become for their descendants,
seven centuries later, not merely a glorious king, but an
emperor, and for the French and Anglo-Normans the centre
of the most adventurous circle of knights that the world had
ever seen.

3

THE INTERMEDIARIES

A PERUSAL of the previous chapter leads inevitably to the conclusion that some powerful forces had been at work between the eleventh and the thirteenth centuries to transform Arthur from an insular into an international figure, from the subject of a purely Welsh and Cornish legend into a king whose literary fame rivalled that of Charlemagne, even in France itself. It is the function of this chapter to determine what these forces were.

Though the problem has been confused by plausible guesses and unwarranted claims, the evidence points clearly to two main agents in the establishment of Arthur's prestige and the popularization outside Celtic lands of what is called the Matter of Britain. The first was the wide-ranging activity of professional Breton story-tellers, *conteurs*, who, speaking French, were welcomed as entertainers wherever that language was understood. The second was the sensation produced by the *History of the Kings of Britain* of Geoffrey of Monmouth, first, in its Latin form, among the learned, and then, in French translation, among the courtly classes.

It will be remembered that in the course of the Anglo-Saxon occupation of what was to be England, thousands of Britons fled from their island home southwards across the sea, and there in what is now called Brittany their descendants multiplied and flourished. Through contact with their French-speaking neighbours many of them became bilingual. They still kept in touch, though, with their cousins, the Welsh and Cornish, across the Channel, and as the Arthurian legend developed and expanded in Wales into a multitude of such prose tales as *Kulhwch*, so the Bretons took them up. A class of wandering minstrels, with histrionic talents, found that this novel material captivated barons and their ladies, not only in Brittany but wherever French was understood. More and more they adapted the fantastic tales to French tastes, manners, and standards of rationality, costumed their characters according to the latest mode, and introduced all the pageantry of chivalry. Their audiences, somewhat bored by a monotonous diet of epics dealing with the quarrels and wars of Charlemagne and his paladins, were fascinated by the new and various tales of love and marvel and adventure, and were easily persuaded to accept the Breton image of Arthur as the nonpareil of kings.

The Norman Conquest opened up new territory. After 1066 William awarded many fiefs all over England to Breton knights who had helped him on the field of Senlac; and, of course, in these transplanted Breton households, as well as in Anglo-Norman halls, the Breton entertainers were welcome. It was thus by way of Brittany that Arthur returned, as it were, to reconquer the land of his historic exploits and become a hero for the Anglo-Normans. And it was as a result of the enormous popularity enjoyed by the Breton tales told in French that we find French romances of Arthur and his knights rendered into Welsh, as we saw in the last chapter; namely, *Geraint*, the *Lady of the Fountain*, and *Peredur*.

There is a rival theory which at first glance seems very plausible. After 1066 there were many direct contacts between the Anglo-Normans and the Welsh, especially in South Wales, and relations were sometimes friendly. What more natural and even inevitable than that tales resembling *Kulhwch* should be transmitted directly across the border to England, without any Breton intermediaries? But so far no one has produced contemporary testimony to direct transmission of Arthurian stories from the Welsh to the Anglo-Normans; there is no close affinity between *Kulhwch* and the Four Branches of the Mabinogi, on the one hand, and Anglo-Norman and Middle

English romances, on the other; and these last, most of them derived from French sources, betray in their nomenclature traces of Breton transmission

To be sure, a certain story-teller named Bleheris or Breri (Welsh Bleddri) enjoyed a prodigious reputation, both in Britain and in France, for his tales of Gawain, the Round Table, and the Grail, and it seems that, having become expert in French, he excelled the Bretons at their own game. But it is unlikely that he ever committed his tales to parchment, and it is impossible to find, even in the French poems which cite his authority, any strain of pure Welsh tradition. The solitary instance of Bleheris does not disprove the preponderant share of the Breton minstrels in the dissemination of Arthurian matter both on the Continent and in England. This oral tradition continued well into the thirteenth century, long after French writers had been busy drawing on this reservoir of story for their own experiments in prose and verse. In brief, the Breton *conteurs* were the direct inspirers, the immediate progenitors, of French Arthurian romance. Once grasp this fact, and you have the answer to many puzzles.

Geoffrey of Monmouth, mentioned in Chapter 2, was the second great intermediary between the Celtic peoples and the non-Celts in spreading the renown of Arthur. The latest authorities believe that he was born of Breton parents who had settled at Monmouth, and that he obtained an excellent education, probably at Oxford, which, though not yet the seat of a university, was already attracting scholars. He was certainly living there between 1129 and 1151, and, as the title *magister* suggests, may have been himself a sort of classics don. Ordained a priest in 1152, he was promptly elevated to the bishopric of St Asaph in North Wales. In 1153 he witnessed at Westminster a charter assuring to Henry of Anjou the succession to the English throne, and in 1155 he died. His literary patrons and presumably his friends were two successive bishops of Lincoln and the powerful illegitimate son of Henry I, Robert Earl of Gloucester. Evidently Geoffrey was on familiar terms with some of the highest ecclesiastical and political figures of his day.

Though Geoffrey was destined to wear the mitre, he never displayed any religious feeling nor any deep concern about the Church. He was ambitious, as his flattering dedications prove; and he was quite unscrupulous, for the *History of the Kings of Britain*, which he claimed to have translated from an ancient book imported from Brittany, was one of the world's most brazen and successful frauds.

Shortly before completing it, he indulged in another piece of mystification, a little book in Latin containing alleged prophecies of Merlin. For centuries previous a poet named Myrddin had been famous in Wales as a soothsayer, and his reputation had spread to Anglo-Norman circles. About 1134 Geoffrey set out to satisfy curiosity about the mage, and boldly composed a set of predictions, not only covering in cryptic style the period up to his own time but also extending into a future filled with lurid catastrophes. Merlin's prediction about Arthur shows that Geoffrey had at least sketched in his mind a glorious career of conquest for the British hero. 'The Boar of Cornwall shall bring succour [to the Britons] and shall trample the necks [of the Saxons] under his feet. The islands of the ocean shall be subdued to his power, and he shall possess the forests of Gaul. The house of Romulus shall dread his fierceness, and his end shall be doubtful. In the mouths of peoples he shall be celebrated, and his deeds shall be food to the tellers of tales.' Highly significant are the cautious remark about the possibility of Arthur's survival and the reference to story-tellers who found in him a subject which provided them with their daily bread.

When, about 1136, Geoffrey completed and published the *History* he included the *Prophecies of Merlin* as the seventh book. In the preface to the larger work he again alluded to the deeds of Arthur and other kings of Britain as proclaimed by many peoples from memory. He then cites as his source an old book in the British language, dealing with these kings, from Brutus, the first, to Cadwalader, the last. If there was any such ancient tome, Geoffrey could not have taken much from it—at most, the names of apocryphal early British rulers, such as Leir; but the story of King Leir and his daughters is Geoffrey's own clever remodelling of the Buddhist parable of a man and his three friends which reached the West in the eleventh century as part of *Barlaam and Josaphat*. Needless to say, the *History* contains a considerable amount of veracious chronicling when the material is drawn from Julius Caesar, Bede, Henry of Huntingdon, etc. But even when Geoffrey had reliable material he used it with cynical ingenuity to create fiction. When he composed his elaborate description of Arthur's second coronation at Caerleon-on-Usk, and found that Welsh Arthurian tradition, as known to him, did not supply enough names of guests for so august an occasion, he picked at random names from ancient Welsh genealogies. And when he could find no record of the kings who succeeded Arthur he arbitrarily took the names from Gildas's invective against several kings reigning simultaneously in Britain, and strung them along seriatim.

It is interesting to observe what the wily 'historian' did with Nennius. From that source Geoffrey lifted the meagre notion that the first conqueror and colonizer of Albion was a Trojan named Brutus, and he then proceeded to stretch it out into a prose *Aeneid*, with Brutus as the hero. The story of Vortigern's tower and the clairvoyant boy also came from Nennius. Geoffrey arbitrarily identified the boy with the youthful Merlin. The name of Uther Pendragon is known to genuine Welsh tradition, but it was probably the misinterpretation of a passage in Nennius which led Geoffrey to make him the father of Arthur. The battles with the Saxons derive from the same source, but their number has been reduced from twelve to three, and these have been treated with much imaginary detail and with much attention to the geography of the campaign. For the supreme victory of Badon, arbitrarily equated with Bath, Arthur armed himself with his shield Pridwen, the sword Caliburn, and the spear Ron—names derived more or less directly from Wales. Apparently to avoid monotony, Geoffrey inserted in the midst of this campaigning an account from Nennius of the marvels of Loch Lomond and of a Welsh whirlpool.

Three of the most important elements in Arthur's career Geoffrey derived from the oral tradition of the *conteurs*, though he may well have met them in written form. For the begetting of the future conqueror by Uther on Gorlois's wife in Tintagel castle he found ready to his hand a local Cornish legend. As for the great climax, Arthur's victory over the Emperor Lucius Hiberus and the legions of Rome, and as for Gawain's (Walwanus's) part in it, there is evidence that an old Welsh tradition of a war between Arthur and his vassal Lluch, of which there are other traces, came to Geoffrey in a Breton-French form. Quite arbitrarily he exalted Lluch to the imperial throne in order to make Arthur's triumph the more splendid. The ironic reversal of fortune, the treachery of Modred, Arthur's nephew, the forced marriage of Guenevere, the pursuit of Modred into Cornwall, and the fatal battle on the River Camel—all this, we may safely believe, represents the tradition which had grown up about the battle of Camlann, first recorded, as we know, in the *Annals of Wales*. To the statement that even the renowned King Arthur was mortally wounded, Geoffrey added the contradictory belief of the Bretons that he was borne away to the isle of Avalon for the healing of his wounds. Evidently on the burning issue of Arthur's survival the Oxford scholar could be quoted on either side. However ardently his Breton friends desired Arthur's messianic return, his Anglo-Norman patrons would find it embarrassing.

Literary and traditional sources provided the great bulk of Geoffrey's matter, but he drew some scenes from life. There can be little doubt that his description of the coronation ceremony at Caerleon and the sports which followed was a clever adaptation of the festivities at the crowning of King Stephen. And most striking is this addition: 'The women . . . esteemed no one worthy of their love but such as had given proof of their valour in three several battles. . . . Thus the ladies were made chaste and the knights more noble because of their love. . . . The knights engaged in a game on horseback in imitation of a battle; the ladies, looking on from the top of the walls, excited in them wild flames of love as is customary in such sports.' Here, then, is the first reference in England to a tournament, the first reference to ladies 'whose bright eyes rain influence and judge the prize', and, even more momentous, the earliest assertion in medieval literature that love between the sexes was an ennobling and refining force. Not that this faker of history was the inventor of what we may call romantic love, any more than he invented the tournament, but evidently he believed in making Arthur's court a mirror of the latest fashions in sport and sentiment.

The more one studies the *History of the Kings of Britain* and the methods of its composition, the more one is astonished at the author's impudence, and the more one is impressed with his cleverness, his art. Written in a polished but not ornate style, displaying sufficient harmony with learned authorities and accepted traditions, free from the wilder extravagances of the *conteurs*, founded ostensibly on a very ancient manuscript, no wonder Geoffrey's *magnum opus* disarmed scepticism and was welcomed by the learned world. To be sure, at the end of the twelfth century William of Newburgh, with extraordinary perspicacity, accused Geoffrey of disguising under the honourable name of history the fables about Arthur which he took from the ancient fictions of the Britons and augmented out of his own head, and of writing to please the Bretons, of whom the majority are said to be so brutishly stupid that they look still for Arthur as if he would return, and will not listen to anyone who says that he is dead. But few readers of Geoffrey's *History* had such acumen. The kings of England could be grateful to a historian who provided them with a predecessor who had conquered all of western Europe except Spain, and whose ancestors, Belinus, Constantine, and Maximian, had seized even Rome itself. For three and a half centuries the *History of the Kings of Britain* was accepted as authoritative, not only in England but on the Continent as well. Manuscripts multiplied; translations were made into Welsh, French, and Norwegian. Contrary to the claims of some scholars, it had very little influence on the French romances of the twelfth century; indeed, the gap in matter and manner between the *History* and the poems could hardly be wider. Only in the French prose romances of the thirteenth century did Geoffrey's version of Arthur's birth, the war with Rome, and the final struggle with Modred exert a strong influence on fiction.

About fifteen years after the launching of his great hoax, Geoffrey composed a poem in Latin hexameters, the *Life of Merlin*, and disclosed not only an easy competence in verse but also a remarkable sympathy with the sufferings of the crazed bard in the Forest of Caledon and a feeling for beauty. For Merlin's story he drew heavily on Welsh traditions, such as those preserved in Welsh poems, but it was a Breton tradition of Arthur's departure to the isle of Avalon and his sojourn there that inspired a very charming passage, put in the mouth of the poet Taliesin.

> The Island of Apples, which men call the Fortunate Isle, is so named because it produces all things without toil. The fields there have no need of farmers to plough them, and Nature alone provides the tilling. Grain and grapes are produced without tending, and apple-trees grow in the woods from the close-clipped grass. . . . Thither, after the battle of Camlan, we brought the wounded Arthur. . . . We arrived there with the Prince, and Morgen received us with suitable honours. In her own chamber she placed the King on a golden bed, with her own noble hand uncovered the wound, and gazed at it long. At last she said that health could return to him if he would stay with her for a long time and was willing to accept the benefits of her healing art. Rejoicing, therefore, we committed the King to her, and, returning, gave our sails to the favouring winds.

Though there are reminiscences here of the Fortunate Isles,

due to Geoffrey's classical learning, it is the island elysium of the Celts to which Arthur comes, not, as in the *Spoils of Annwn*, as the head of a band of raiders, but alone, the victim of Modred's treachery, to be cured by the presiding goddess of the isle, known to us from Malory as Morgan le Fay.

To the few who have read Geoffrey's *Life of Merlin* it may well seem the author's most attractive and artistic work, but it made only a ripple when it was tossed into the literary stream, whereas the *History of the Kings of Britain* started a great wave. In 1155 a Norman poet, Wace, completed a free and spirited paraphrase in couplets, called the *Brut*, and presented a copy to Eleanor of Aquitaine, the new Queen of England. This French version, of course, extended the knowledge of Geoffrey's book to the courtly classes, and much of its interest lies in the methods Wace used to adapt the narrative to this new audience by toning down the barbarities, adding picturesque detail, and giving costumes, customs, and combats a very up-to-date air. Interesting, too, to the literary historian are the references to the *conteurs* and their ways, and to the Round Table, 'of which the Bretons tell many tales'. It was given this shape, says Wace, in order to prevent quarrels over precedence. All the barons were seated on an equality and were served equally. In Wace's day the table of the Last Supper, at which Christ sat with his twelve disciples, was believed to be round, and this concept probably influenced his account, but a Celtic tradition of chiefs or kings seated at banquets with twelve warriors in a circle around them was probably the nucleus from which Arthur's celebrated table developed.

The earliest English poem in which Arthur figures was an expanded rendering of Wace made by one Layamon (or Lawman), a priest of Arley Regis, Worcestershire, shortly before or shortly after 1200. He wrote, naturally, in the alliterative tradition of English poetry, though in a verse-form less strict than that of the great Anglo-Saxon classics, and there is an increasing use of rime or assonance as the poem proceeds, probably due to the influence of Wace's couplets. The vocabulary is overwhelmingly Anglo-Saxon. The nickers that haunt Grendel's mere in *Beowulf* bathe in Layamon's Loch Lomond. There are *scops* in both poems, and there is *dream* (revelry) in hall. Both poets, though Christian, accept the idea of inexorable doom implied in the Saxon word *faege*, Middle English *feye*, Scots *fey*. There is a remarkable correspondence to *Beowulf* in the fact that the Anglo-Saxon hero wears a white helmet and a corselet forged by Wayland the Smith, whereas Arthur, preparing for the battle of Bath, donned a helmet named 'Goose-white' and a corselet wrought by an elvish smith.

While Wace rendered Geoffrey's narrative more lively and graphic by elaborate descriptions of the festivities at Arthur's coronation and of the embarkation of his army at Southampton, Layamon emphasized the dramatic and emotional effects. Indirect discourse becomes direct, and similes, rare in Anglo-Saxon poetry, convey not only an image but also feeling. This is the exultant speech of Arthur after the surrender of Childric's army at the wood of Calidon:

'Thanked be the Lord, who deals out all dooms, that Childric the strong is weary of my land! My land he portioned out to all his knights; myself he planned to drive out of my country, to hold me for a weakling and to have my kingdom. . . . But to him it has happened as with the fox when he is boldest over the weald and has his fill of sport and fowls aplenty. Friskily he climbs and seeks the crags, works himself holes in the wilderness, and wherever he may fare has never a care. He thinks that in bravery he is the boldest of beasts. But then men from the valley come towards him with horns, with hounds, with loud cries. Hunters there shout, hounds there bay, and drive the fox over dales and over downs. He flees to the hill, seeks his hole, and creeps into the farthest end. Then is the bold fox bereft of all bliss. Men dig towards him on every side. Then is most wretched the proudest of all beasts. So was it with Childric, the strong and the rich!'

There is nothing of this in Wace, nor of Arthur's later speech at the battle of Bath, in which he likened the corpses of the Saxons lying in the River Avon to steel fishes. Strange that a Saxon poet should exult at length and with such gusto over the triumphs of his ancestral foes; strange, too, that these elaborate similes are found nowhere in Layamon's long poem except in this part dealing with the Saxon war. What can be the explanation? It has been recently and plausibly argued that Layamon must have had an unknown source for these expansions of Wace's narrative. An Anglo-Norman poet, it would seem, was more likely to indulge in these scornful comparisons than a descendant of the people scorned. Still the puzzle remains: why did Layamon enjoy them and reproduce them?

Besides these few longish similes and the many expansions prompted by striving for pictorial and dramatic effect, there are four additions surely derived from other sources than Wace. When Arthur, after defeating the Roman emperor Lucius, was about to set forth for the capture of Rome, he dreamed that he was sitting astride the roof of a hall, with Gawain before him. Modred came with a battle-axe and hewed in pieces the posts which upheld the building, and Guenevere pulled down the roof, so that Arthur fell and broke his right arm. Gripping his sword with his left hand, he cut off Modred's head so that it rolled on the floor, and he hacked the Queen to pieces. Since there exist other versions of Arthur's portentous dream, including Malory's, the theme must have been traditional.

To Wace's passage about the founding of the Round Table, at which all Arthur's knights sat on an equality, Layamon made some striking additions. At a high feast in the presence of the King and Queen a fierce brawl broke out over precedence in seating, and was quelled only after bloodshed. The beginner of the fracas Arthur doomed to death, as well as all his male kin, and his female kin were condemned to lose their noses. Soon after, a Cornish carpenter built a round table, large enough to accommodate sixteen hundred and more, yet light enough to be carried wherever Arthur rode. Thereafter there were no quarrels about seating. Since Layamon goes on to say that this is the board of which the Bretons (*Bruttes*) boast, there is little reason to doubt that the story was of Breton origin.

Surely of Breton provenance were the brief passages about Arthur's birth and his passing to Avalon. When his mother Igerne was delivered, fays (*alven*) took the child and bestowed on him with mighty spells the gifts of strength, dominion, long life, and generosity. And at last, wounded in his battle with Modred, he told his successor that he was about to fare to Avalon, to the loveliest of fays, Argante the Queen, who would make him all whole; and then he would come again to his kingdom and dwell with the Britons with great joy. 'Even with the words, there came from the sea a short boat gliding, driven by the waves, and two women in it, wondrously clad; they took Arthur anon, and quickly bore him, and laid him down softly, and moved away. . . . The Bretons believe yet that he is alive and dwells in Avalon with the fairest of all fays.'

The four additions which have just been pointed out, though borrowed from other sources, nevertheless reveal something of Layamon himself: his admiration for Arthur as a stern and just king; his acceptance of magic and the supernatural. But we also discover a strain of ferocity which is absent from Wace. Arthur was regarded, of course, by both poets as a model Christian: before battle he calls on God and St Mary for aid; Layamon endows him with a sense of sportsmanship which prevents him from attacking the giant of Mont St Michel while he is asleep. But there is too a Nazi streak of ruthlessness and cruelty in Layamon, which cannot be overlooked. Arthur threatens to burn his wife Guenevere, and the gallant Gawain proposes to have her torn to pieces by horses.

In spite of this repulsive element, the English *Brut* is a great poem, epic in scope, high of mood, pulsating with vitality, and in many passages generous and tender.

4

CHRÉTIEN DE TROYES

As we have just seen, the celebrity of Arthur, established throughout western Christendom and in the Crusader states by the end of the twelfth century, was due, first, to the French-speaking Breton *conteurs*, and, secondly, to the work of Geoffrey of Monmouth and its adaptation by Wace. The *conteurs* won an audience by the verve of their recital and the emotional appeal of their stories, often, as we learn from contemporary testimony, moving their listeners to tears. Geoffrey and Wace impressed the learned and sceptical by their specious claim to historicity. About 1170 or a little before, a poet, Chrétien de Troyes, began his literary career and produced five longish romances in octosyllabic couplets which added enormously to the vogue of Arthurian story. They produced in aristocratic circles throughout western Europe and Italy a sensation comparable to that of the Waverley novels, and were still being copied in the fourteenth century, and translated into modern prose in the fifteenth.

Of Chrétien's life we know only what can be inferred from his writings. If not born at Troyes, he must have long resided at that flourishing commercial town, the seat of the counts of Champagne. He was schooled in Latin, for he began by making translations from Ovid (of which only one has survived), and he practised some of the precepts found in the Latin manuals of rhetoric. His poem *Cligès* shows such an accurate knowledge of the positions of Southampton, Winchester, Wallingford, Windsor, etc., as only a visit to southern England can account for. He moved in very high society, for *Lancelot* was composed for Marie, Countess of

Champagne, and *Perceval* was commissioned by Philip, Count of Flanders, at one time Regent of France. Chrétien was proudly aware that France in his day had achieved that pre-eminence in war, learning, and letters which in ancient times had been held by Greece and Rome. He himself carried on the classical tradition not only by his adaptations of Ovid but also by his stylistic imitations of the long French epics on classical subjects, *Thèbes* and *Enéas*, which had been fashionable in the decades preceding his own poetic activity. But he chose to devote his matured talents to the Matter, not of Rome, but of Britain.

Of his five Arthurian romances *Cligès* was the second in order of composition, but since it was his most original work, let us consider it first. He claimed, to be sure, that his material came from a book in the library of Beauvais Cathedral, but he shows the influence of so many different works that we may safely classify this alleged source with Geoffrey of Monmouth's Breton manuscript and Chatterton's Rowley parchments. Following the precedent set by the poet Thomas in his *Tristan*, Chrétien devoted the first part of *Cligès* to his hero's father, Alexandre, son of the Emperor of Constantinople, who, attracted by the fame of Arthur's court, sailed to Britain, fell in love with Gawain's sister, and, after distinguishing himself by the capture of Windsor Castle, married her. Of this union Cligès was born. In the course of time his grandfather and father died, and he became the rightful heir to the throne. His uncle, however, forestalled him, and in violation of a pledge sought to marry the Emperor of Germany's daughter, Fénice. Before the nuptials took place at Cologne, she fell in love with Cligès, and he with her. She resolved never to submit, as Iseut did, to the embraces of a husband she did not love; so, thanks to a philtre prepared by her duenna, she was able to delude her husband and remain a virgin. Ignorant of this trick and of Fénice's sentiments towards him, Cligès departed to Britain and took part incognito in a tournament on a plain near Oxford. (Did the poet have Port Meadow in mind?) Such was his prowess that he hurled even Lancelot and Perceval from their saddles. When he returned to Greece, he learned from Fénice the true state of affairs. To gain her freedom, she, like Juliet, drank a potion which rendered her lifeless and was laid in a grave. Unlike Juliet, she was safely removed by her lover to a tower, where she revived and lived with him blissfully for some months. Discovered, they escaped to Britain. When, opportunely, the usurping emperor went mad and died, the lovers returned to Greece to be wedded and crowned. 'Of his mistress he made his wife, but he still called her mistress and lady, and she did not lose anything by it, for he loved her as his mistress, and she, too, loved him as a woman ought to love her lover.'

This summary does not reveal the stylistic devices and the elaborate use of soliloquy, imitated from Ovid and the *Enéas*, by which Chrétien sympathetically analysed the sentiments of his lovers. Indeed, so delicate and subtle is his method that he might be called the Richardson of French medieval romance. Here is a passage from Fénice's monologue of 165 lines:

'With what intent could Cligès say to me, "I am all yours," unless love made him say it? How can I be his superior, why should he prize me so highly that he should make me the mistress of his heart? Is he not fairer than I and of higher degree? I see nothing but love that could grant me this gift. I, who cannot escape its power, will prove by my own case that, if he did not love me, he would never call himself mine. Nor would I be wholly his nor would I say so if love had not placed me in his power, nor would Cligès say in any way that he was all mine if love did not hold him in its bonds. For if he does not love me, he does not hold me in awe. Love, which gives me wholly to him, will, I hope, give him to me in return. But it frightens me utterly that it is a common phrase, and I may be soon deceived. For there are those who flatteringly say even to strangers: "I and all that I have are yours," and their talk is as empty as a jay's. So I do not know what to trust, for it might well be that he said it to deceive me.

But I saw his colour change and I saw him weeping piteously. The tears, to my thinking, and his abashed and wretched mien were never feigned, nor was there falsehood there. The eyes from which I saw the tears fall did not lie. I saw signs enough of love, if I know anything about it.'

Thus delicately and realistically Chrétien traced the alternations of hope and fear in the heart of his heroine.

All students of Chrétien recognize the powerful influence of the Tristan story on *Cligès*, though differing as to the version he knew. He seems to have found nothing to condemn in the illicit passion of the lovers and their treatment of Mark, though he blamed Iseut severely for cohabiting with both husband and lover—a situation common even in Christian societies when the *mariage de convenance* is the rule, and the love-match the exception. The poet created in Fénice a heroine bold enough to seek a way of escape from such a repulsive situation. One may object that her way, though possible in poetry, was far from practicable in life. Nevertheless, Chrétien deserves our respect for seeing the humiliation and the debasement of character that went with the *ménage à trois*.

In *Cligès*, then, Chrétien revealed himself, his tastes, his talents, his ideals. He manifested a strong bent towards realism. To be sure, the philtre which deluded the Emperor is unknown to science, but otherwise everything that happens in the poem lies within the range of possibility. Every geographical name can be found on a map, and the feelings of the characters are natural.

What a strange contrast is presented by Chrétien's next poem, *Lancelot* or the *Knight of the Cart*. It has been called a palinode, a recantation, since it seems to glorify the adulterous passion of Lancelot for Guenevere. It assigns to Arthur, in *Cligès* the paragon of kings, the inglorious role of a cuckold. Of the five regions or places where the action occurs—

Logres (England), Bade (Bath), Camelot, Goirre, and Noauz
—the last three belong to the geography of dreams. To the
world of fantasy likewise belong the adventures of the perilous
bed and of the sword which serves as a bridge to the land of
Goirre. Lancelot's abject submission to the whims of the
Queen exceeds the bounds of the credible, and the fabric
of the plot is full of loose ends. How is one to explain this
radical change in matter and manner? Let me first summarize
the story.

When Arthur was holding court at Camelot, Meleagant,
prince of the water-girdled land of Goirre, appeared and
boasted that he held captive many of Arthur's subjects (later
identified as the people of Logres). He challenged the King to
send the Queen out under the escort of one of his knights, and
promised that, if defeated by this knight, he would release all
the captives. Arthur, bound by a rash promise, meekly allowed
Kay to take up the challenge and ride out with the Queen.
In the ensuing combat, Meleagant overcame the seneschal
and led both him and the lady away. Later he unhorsed even
Lancelot. Thus it was that Gawain, setting out to the rescue,
came on Lancelot walking behind a cart. The driver told
Lancelot to get in if he would have news of the Queen. Lancelot,
torn between his pride and his love for Guenevere, hesitated for
two steps before mounting. Thereafter, however, he passed
every test of his devotion and prowess. That night, though
warned, he insisted on sleeping in a perilous bed, and narrowly
escaped being pierced by a fiery lance. Another night, an
amorous chatelaine lay down beside him, but he turned his
back on her. He lifted the marble lid of a sarcophagus—a feat
reserved for the deliverer of the people of Logres. He crawled
across a long sword-bridge, cutting his hands, knees, and feet.
Arrived in the land of Goirre, he carried to preposterous
lengths that love-service which Geoffrey of Monmouth mentioned fleetingly as a characteristic of Arthur's knights. He
fought Meleagant back-handed so that he might gaze up at his
lady watching from a tower. When he came into her presence
after the combat she treated him with scorn. Why? Because he

had hesitated for a moment to mount the cart. (How she knew this, except by telepathy, we cannot guess.) At the tourney of Noauz she put him to an extreme test. For two days at her command he played the coward and allowed himself to be chased about. Only on the third day did she relent, and command him to do his best, whereupon he swept the field. In short, Lancelot's passion is an idolatry. Finally in a duel at Arthur's court he killed Meleagant and restored Guenevere to her ineffectual husband.

It would be hard to believe that this poem was written by the author of *Cligès* unless we had the poet's word and the poet's explanation, namely, that the Countess of Champagne gave him the story (*matière*) and the dominant idea (*sen*). As for the narrative material most critics would agree that it is largely drawn from Celtic sources and that it must have reached Chrétien in the somewhat disordered state which it takes in the poem. Certainly, as a schoolgirl once wrote, Arthur's queen was 'a lady very much subject to the misfortune of being run away with'; and that this tradition antedated Chrétien by several decades at least is proved by a brief account in the *Life of St Gildas* of her abduction by Melvas, King of the Summer Country, and her eventual rescue by Arthur. Behind the tradition lay a myth of the Persephone type, with this important difference, that Guenevere was not carried down to a gloomy Hades, but to an elysian Isle of Glass (*Voirre*). In *Lancelot* the Isle of Glass can be recognized in the water-girdled land of Goirre (a scribal corruption of *Voirre*), even though little is left of its elysian nature.

The myth of Guenevere's abduction is by no means the only traditional theme in the poem. Investigation has shown, for instance, Irish origins for the episodes of the cart, the perilous bed, and the sword-bridge. Lancelot himself, as noted in Chapter 1, may be traced back through the Welsh warrior Lluch Llaunnauc of the early Welsh poems to the Irish divinity Lugh Lamhfada. Those who know him solely in the French and English versions of his career and think of him only in his relations with the Queen may well feel that this is a rash claim, for there is no Guenevere in the life of Lugh. But the Swiss poet, Ulrich von Zatzikhoven, ekes out our knowledge of the Lancelot tradition by his translation from a lost Anglo-Norman romance about the hero, so that one can point to eight correspondences between him and his Irish prototype, Lugh. At least one scene, in which Lancelot forces the bars of a window, and lies with the Queen, leaving blood-stains on the bed, Chrétien may have borrowed from some version of the Tristan romance. The poem, then, is largely a patchwork of ancient and incongruous elements, and Chrétien did not succeed in reducing them to harmony and coherence. One may suspect that he did not try too hard. It cannot be proved that his reason for leaving the conclusion to Godefroi de Lagny to compose was that he wanted to be relieved of an uncongenial task, but that seems a plausible motive.

The origin of the *matière* is not hard to determine, though complete agreement on the subject will never be attained. The precise nature of the *sen*, the controlling idea, which the Countess Marie required the poet to express through the *matière*, presents a subtle problem. Though it is obvious that Lancelot exemplifies an ideal of amatory conduct by his idolatrous, even sacrilegious, attitude towards his lady, and that this is the *sen* of the poem, did Marie wish us to take that ideal seriously or to find it absurd? In other words, did she command Chrétien to treat Lancelot with admiration or irony?

Hitherto the prevailing opinion has held that the Countess was something of a propagandist for what has been called '*amour courtois*'. Andreas Capellanus, a contemporary and possibly a chaplain attached to her court, depicts her as rendering decisions on questions of love, and quotes a letter, supposedly written in 1174, in which she declares flatly that love cannot exist between husband and wife, since their relations are governed by contract and not by spontaneous choice. She goes on to recommend to married women the service of love outside the bounds of wedlock, and asserts that her opinion is supported by a great many ladies. Both Andreas and Chrétien seem to agree, then, in ascribing to the Countess of Champagne an outspoken advocacy of adultery as the only true love.

Though this interpretation of her views has long been accepted, it has been questioned in late years, for there are two difficulties. Can we reconcile it with what we know of her life and reputation? The daughter of the King of France, Louis VII, and Eleanor of Aquitaine, she was married to Count Henry of Champagne in 1159 or shortly before. Though dismissed by her husband temporarily for cause unknown, she was received back into favour in 1164 and thereafter enjoyed a spotless reputation. On his death in 1181 she was sought in marriage by Count Philip of Flanders. She commissioned a poetic version of Genesis with commentary. All this is hardly compatible with the notion that Marie was an open advocate of marital infidelity, a propagandist for doctrines subversive not only of feudal loyalties but also of the sacramental system.

A second difficulty is to be found in Chrétien's treatment of Lancelot. Was it intended to be serious, or was it intended as burlesque? Again scholarly opinion has tended to shift from the former alternative to the latter. Few modern readers would deny that there is deliberate exaggeration in the lengths to which Lancelot's frenzy carries him and in the humiliations to which he meekly submits. Having found beside a spring a comb in which some strands of the Queen's hair were caught, he almost swoons, then presses the hairs a hundred thousand times to his eyes, mouth, and forehead, before depositing them under his shirt next the heart. Another time he is so lost in contemplation of his lady that he is challenged three times by a knight and is hurled from his horse into a ford before he comes to himself. Later, on hearing a false report of Guenevere's death, he attempts suicide, by fitting his neck into a noose, attaching the noose firmly to his saddle-bow, and letting himself fall. It seems that many medieval readers, including the author of the *Prose Lancelot*, took these aberrancies rather solemnly, but Chrétien was far too sane. His Lancelot is a caricature, a Don Quixote. That this was what the

Countess also intended may be questioned, but the probability is that she and the poet understood each other.

What was it that Chrétien was caricaturing? Here there can be little doubt: it was the religion of love which for about a century had gradually spread through the literary circles of southern France. Its exponents were the troubadours of the Limousin, Poitou, Aquitaine, the Toulousain, and Provence. They wrote in a common professional tongue; their verse-forms were varied and called for extreme technical virtuosity. Their subjects might be war, or satire, or politics, but love was far and away the favourite theme. Never marital love, nor was the object normally marriage. The *alba*, or dawn-song, dealt with the parting of lovers after a night of clandestine enjoyment; the *pastorela* with the amorous advances of a knight to a shepherd girl. But most of the troubadour lyrics breathe a sublimated passion, lasting, all-absorbing, often unrequited. The lady is a being exalted by her beauty high above her languishing slave. She is an inspiration to liberality and courage. 'Through Love the haughty become humble, the base are ennobled, the lazy become skilled, and the foolish wise.'

This *fin amor*, as it was called, this woman-worship, was revolutionary in two respects. It defied the teachings of the Church and the conventions of society by rejecting marriage, as then determined by property and pedigree, and substituting a relationship based on free choice. It defied Church and society by giving woman a higher worth and a superior status to man's. This was a very natural revolt. There is no blinking the fact that most feudal marriages represented a financial or political bargain, and often the bargain was made when the bridegroom and the bride were twelve years old or under. As Benjamin Franklin observed: 'Where there is marriage without love, there will be love without marriage.' Both Church and society were agreed that the female sex was inferior to the male. Made of Adam's rib, Eve brought about his fall and so the fall of all mankind; and Eve's daughters were notorious for following the example of their mother. So spake the

Church, though making exception for virgin martyrs and holy women. As to the civil and domestic status of women, the medieval handicaps have not all been removed yet. It must have given a profound joy to women of spirit when, instead of being reminded continually of their sins and their subject state, they were adored by their poet lovers and credited with every virtue.

Of course, other forces went to the shaping of the cult of *fin amor*. The list of them is fairly long, and one, often proposed, is the cult of the Queen of Heaven, which was already a formidable rival to the worship of the Trinity. Plausible as this hypothesis may seem, there is an objection. The south of France was a hotbed of heresy, the first troubadour was ex-communicated, and *fin amor* was directed towards another man's wife. Is this the milieu in which the very pious cult of the Virgin would have had a great influence? Doubtless, at a later period there was some interplay, some exchange of imagery and modes of expression, between the adorers of the heavenly Mary and the adorers of earthly Marys and Marians and Margarets. But religious influence on troubadour poetry is singularly lacking. And when it came to open conflict in the early thirteenth century the Church used its power to crush not only the Albigensian heresy but also the rarefied eroticism which expressed itself in the Provençal lyric.

A theory which has been gaining ground in recent years attributes a large influence on both the poetic form and the ideology of that lyric to the Moors of Spain. Every medieval scholar recognizes the great debt which the West owed to Arabic science and philosophy, and it is increasingly realized how prosperous and refined was the society of Moorish Spain in the eleventh and twelfth centuries. And in spite of inter-mittent wars, and partly because of them, there was a flow of cultural influences to the north. It is therefore no accident that we find in the literature of Moslem Spain metrical forms approximating those of the troubadours, and similar conven-tions such as that of addressing the mistress as 'my lord', in Provençal 'midons'. Most significant is the fact that a book called the *Dove's Neck-Ring*, written by the Andalusian, Ibn Hazm, about 1022, might almost serve as a textbook on *fin amor*, so close are its idealistic doctrines on all points—except one. The object of one's adoration must not be married. But, as from the troubadours, one learns from Ibn Hazm that under the influence of love, many a stingy one becomes generous, a gloomy one becomes bright-faced, a coward becomes brave, a curmudgeon gay, and an ignoramus clever. It is hard to avoid the conclusion that the literature of southern Spain had a profound effect on the literature of southern France, which, in turn, had a profound effect on the literature of western Christendom, including Italy. The wave of influence swept through the love-poetry of Dante and Petrarch and all their disciples. And, to quote C. S. Lewis: 'French poets in the eleventh century discovered or invented or were the first to express that romantic species of passion which English poets were still writing about in the nineteenth.'

To return to Chrétien, it seems most likely that at the command of his patroness he deliberately burlesqued the extravagances, the posturings, of certain knightly practitioners of *fin amor*. He performed his task with thoroughness and with a rather obvious humour. Apparently, though, he was too subtle for many readers of his own and the next generation, for they seem to have thought Lancelot the ideal of a lover, even if he was a bit extreme in his idolatry. How else can one explain his appearance, with all his idiosyncrasies, as the hero of the huge prose romance, which remained a 'best-seller' for three hundred years?

It is significant that Chrétien not only poked fun at an adulterous lover but also treated with charm and sympathy love at first sight for a modest and meek maiden, leading promptly to marriage, and surviving the severest of trials. This is, of course, the subject of *Erec*, Chrétien's earliest Arthurian romance. Tennyson so admired its Welsh counterpart, *Geraint*, that he used it as the basis of two of his *Idylls of the King*. Most of the credit for the charm of style and the elaborate treatment of psychology displayed in *Erec* should be assigned to Chrétien; for these are characteristics which point to the author of *Cligès*. But there are other features of *Erec* and *Ivain* which differentiate them from *Cligès* and lead us to surmise that Chrétien was using as the basis of these poems two already well-organized and refined romances. It is not without significance that the heroes of both narratives bear Breton names, while *Erec* contains seven other names of the same origin. Both poems, as we saw in Chapter 2, are paralleled fairly closely by the Welsh *Geraint* and the *Lady of the Fountain*, and, though the matter is the subject of controversy, their relation to the Welsh tales may best be explained by common sources in French. The general resemblance between the plots of *Erec* and *Ivain*—both romances telling of the wooing and winning of a bride, marriage, estrangement, probation, forgiveness, and reconcilement—seems to prove that they were constructed out of traditional material by a single mind, a mind endowed with unusual narrative gifts, but not the mind which created *Cligès*.

The story of *Erec* may be sketched as follows. When one morning King Arthur and his knights had ridden out from Cardigan to chase the White Stag, the Queen followed after, escorted by young Erec, who was armed with only a sword. They met a fully armed knight, named Ider son of Nut (Welsh, Edern son of Nudd), and the Queen sent first her handmaid and then Erec to ask him to come to her, but a dwarf in the service of Ider lashed each of them with a scourge. Erec, unwilling to risk a combat with the knight, nevertheless followed him with intent to avenge the wrong when opportunity offered. He was hospitably entertained by an impoverished vavasour, and fell promptly in love with his lovely daughter Enide. Provided with arms by his host, he vanquished Ider the next day in a contest for the prize of a sparrow-hawk, and at the same time vindicated the superior beauty of Enide. He returned with her to Arthur's court, to the delight of all and especially the Queen. The nuptials were attended by many potentates, including such traditional figures as Maheloas, lord of the Isle of Glass (*Voirre*), and Bilis, the dwarf king of the Antipodes. Later Erec carried off the honours in a tournament near Edinburgh (Danebroc), and still later brought his bride to his father's home at Caerwent.

There, steeped in connubial bliss, he abandoned all knightly exercises, so that mutterings began to arise. By ill luck he overheard Enide reproaching herself as the cause of these complaints, and in anger forced her to ride forth with him and forbade her to speak to him unless spoken to. After many trials of his prowess and her fidelity, he demonstrated to her that he was no weakling, and convinced himself of her perfect devotion. A mysterious adventure called the Joy of the Court still awaited him. In a garden enclosed by a wall of air he defeated a tall knight in red arms called Mabonagrain (apparently the solar Mabon of the early Welsh poem), and released him from the sway of his faery mistress. Finally, on the death of his father, Erec was crowned, together with his Enide, at Nantes in Brittany.

A thorough analysis of the narrative materials of *Erec*, as well as a study of the names, proves that, unlike *Cligès*, the poem is a compound of traditional Celtic motifs and patterns. But it is also clear that as the materials reached Chrétien they had been much modified and deftly fitted together to form an unusually coherent and significant design—what the poet himself called a '*mout bele conjointure*'. Presumably, it was the excellence of the general design which led him to undertake a more sophisticated poetic rendering. Apparently, too, the ideas implicit in the plot appealed to him, namely: poverty should be no bar to a true love-match; a newly wedded husband should not be so absorbed in his bride as to let himself grow soft; a wife's patience and courage will prevail over misunderstanding. One may reasonably surmise that it was Chrétien's admiration for the structure and the 'message' of *Erec* which not only prompted him to make his own version, but also to invent an original problem romance, *Cligès*. That his *Erec* was an improvement on his source, excellent as that was, goes without saying. He seems to have felt the need for a stronger conclusion, for the coronation of Erec and Enide at Nantes has every appearance of being added to satisfy this artistic requirement.

The background of *Ivain*, the fourth in order of Chrétien's romances, was much the same as for *Erec*. A résumé will disclose not only a well-constructed plot, in which elements of Celtic derivation are found, but also a similar general outline.

A knight of Arthur's court, Calogrenant, set out to prove his mettle, was pleasantly entertained by a hospitable vavasour and his daughter, met a huge black herdsman, and was directed by him to a perilous spring. When Calogrenant poured water on a large block of emerald a terrific storm arose and a tall knight, guardian of the spring, rode up and overthrew him. When, long after, he told of his humiliation, Ivain son of Urien determined to avenge his cousin. In his turn he met the hospitable host and the giant herdsman, but instead of being unhorsed by the knight of the spring he wounded him mortally and pursued him to his castle. Here, though trapped in a tower by a falling portcullis, Ivain was saved from his enemies by a damsel named Lunete, who in reward for a previous service gave him a ring of invisibility. When his opponent died Ivain had a glimpse of the widow and fell in love with her. Lunete proved equal to this emergency and persuaded the widow, Laudine, that it was her duty to marry Ivain.

After a brief honeymoon he was enticed by Arthur to leave his bride, and Laudine gave consent on condition that he would return within a year. But, in contrast to Erec, he became so absorbed in tournaments that he forgot the day of his return, and in anger Laudine sent a messenger to Arthur's court, who denounced Ivain's faithlessness and forbade him to return. Overwhelmed with grief and shame, he went stark mad, and for a long time roamed the woods naked. He was recognized as he lay asleep and cured by the application of an ointment prepared by Morgan the Wise.

Supplied once more with horse and arms, he delivered a

countess from siege and a lion from a fiery serpent. The noble animal showed its gratitude by bowing before its benefactor, bringing him venison, and guarding him while he slept. On three occasions when Ivain was engaged in combat the lion rushed to the aid of its master, and thus he became known as the Knight of the Lion. Incognito he was involved in a judicial duel with Gawain, also incognito, and of course he could not have had a more formidable antagonist. When at nightfall there was a pause, Ivain learned that he had been shedding the blood of his dearest friend. Each then insisted that he was beaten and yielded the victory to the other. Arthur settled the magnanimous dispute. Lunete, again exercising her wiles on Laudine, persuaded her to marry the Knight of the Lion. When he turned out to be her delinquent husband, Laudine was furious, but relented when he begged her forgiveness, and all ended happily.

The plot, as a moment's consideration will reveal, follows the same general pattern as that of *Erec*—wooing and winning of a beautiful bride, marriage, estrangement, probation, forgiveness, and reconcilement. The parallel is enforced by the neat contrast between Erec, who allowed his wife to distract him from tournaments, and Ivain, who allowed tournaments to distract him from his duties as a husband. The one great flaw, in fact, in Chrétien's treatment of Ivain is his exaggeration of Ivain's fault: the supposedly adoring husband of Laudine leaves his bride soon after the wedding and at the end of a year forgets to return, so obsessed is he with breaking spears. Otherwise the characterization in *Ivain* needs no apology: the loyal, though devious, Lunete; the proud heiress, Laudine, genuinely mourning the death of her husband, but impelled by mixed motives of prudence, concern for her people, and physical attraction to marry within three days her husband's slayer; the lion, which by its human antics and its exemplary gratitude must have appealed strongly to the medieval sense of humour and sense of honour. And, of course, the grateful beast is still, for those who relish Shaw's *Androcles and the Lion*, a major attraction.

After a hundred years of study the sources of *Ivain* have been identified, though, as usual, there is some disagreement. The lion has been traced back through the centuries to the Androcles story. The giant herdsman carries us back to the similar figure in *Kulhwch and Olwen*. Though the hero's name, Ivain, is Breton, it replaces the Welsh Owain, and Owain son of Urien was a historic personage who fought, together with his father, against the Angles who invaded Northumbria in the last quarter of the sixth century. As with Arthur, his exploits endeared him to the Welsh bards of his own and a later generation, and he was drawn into the Arthurian orbit. In the *Dream of Rhonabwy*, let us remember, he appears playing a game with Arthur, and his goddess-mother and her companions take the form of ravens. Indeed, a very primitive legend made him out to be the offspring of Urien and the river-goddess Modron. In the course of time the river-goddess became the fay of a spring, and Owain took the place of his father as her lover. This is why in the Welsh version of Ivain's romance Owain's mistress and wife is called 'the Lady of the Fountain'. But in both the Welsh and the French versions great care has been taken to remove all traces of heathen myth or casual liaison. At a late stage a Breton identified the fountain with the celebrated spring in the Forest of Broceliande, where even in the nineteenth century the peasants, in time of drought, used to pour water on a stone in order to induce rain. And whereas Laudine inherits something from the Welsh goddess Modron, she also inherits through many intermediaries something from the Irish sea-nymph Fand, one of the many loves of the Irish hero Cuchulainn. There is in the whole range of Arthurian literature no piece in which the fusion of Celtic elements is more clear, and in which it has been more successfully carried out.

Let us turn to the last and much the longest of Chrétien's romances, *Perceval*. Though inferior in the later parts to his best work, in others it is hardly excelled in medieval fiction, and as the earliest extant story of the mysterious Grail it will always exercise a peculiar fascination. Neither its merits nor its flaws are to be ascribed wholly to the author himself, for, if we take his word, he found the story ready-made in a book which Philip of Flanders gave him and which he professed merely to turn into rime.

Perceval, or the *Story of the Grail*, may be divided into three parts: the youthful adventures of the hero; his visit to the Grail castle and its sequel; the adventures of Gawain. In the first we read how the orphan boy, brought up by his mother near the base of Snowdon in entire ignorance of the great world, became an expert huntsman with javelins. When he caught sight for the first time of knights in glittering mail, he fell on his knees, thinking they were God and His angels. Being corrected, he inquired about their equipment and its uses, like any modern boy. He set out to find the king 'who made knights', leaving his mother to die of grief. He entered a gay tent, mistaking it for a church, found a damsel within and helped himself to kisses, pasties, and wine. Arrived at Carlisle, he discovered Arthur's court steeped in gloom because a knight in red arms had just claimed Arthur's lands, seized his golden cup, and departed with impunity. Perceval, without waiting to be knighted, rode out, killed the Red Knight with a javelin-cast, took his coat of mail and his weapons, but refused to return to Arthur. A friendly lord, Gornemant by name, entertained the callow youth, instructed him in horsemanship and the use of lance and sword, dubbed him knight, and before his departure charged him not to talk too much, for it was a sin. Next, as the guest of the beautiful chatelaine Blanchefleur, he delivered her castle from a besieging army and spent several days of pleasant dalliance with her before riding away to learn how his mother was faring. All this first part of Perceval's history is a masterpiece of chivalric adventure and light comedy. It justifies the claim which the author made for it, as the best tale ever told in a royal court. Note, however, the ignoble role assigned to Arthur, so sharply contrasted with that of the spirited stripling, Perceval.

The second part is made up of four episodes concerned

with the ever fascinating theme of the Grail. Invited by a nobleman whom he encountered fishing in a river, Perceval entered a castle, to find his host arrived before him, lying on a couch. A procession passed through the hall: a squire bearing a lance from which a drop of blood flowed, two squires bearing candelabra, a beautiful damsel holding a jewel-studded *graal* (a large, somewhat deep platter), and another damsel with a carving dish. Though consumed with curiosity, Perceval remained silent in obedience to Gornemant's command. After the procession had passed out, a sumptuous banquet was served, and at each course the same procession entered and passed out. Still Perceval held his peace. After the lord of the castle had been carried to his chamber Perceval slept in the hall. The next morning he was astonished to find the castle deserted, and rode away.

In the next scene he met his female cousin, and learned from her that his host of the evening before was called the Fisher King, for, maimed in battle by a javelin-thrust through the thighs, he took his diversion in fishing. The damsel rebuked Perceval bitterly for failing to ask about the *graal*, for, had he done so, the King would have been healed. The third scene is laid at Arthur's court at Caerleon. A hideous, maiden messenger rode in on a mule and cursed Perceval for his silence concerning lance and *graal*. Utterly humiliated, Perceval departed to seek the Grail castle and remedy his omission. Throughout these three scenes the atmosphere of mystery is maintained, and the reader, like Perceval, awaits with impatience an explanation of the lance, the two vessels, and the hideous damsel.

In the fourth scene we are offered a partial explanation. Five years later on Good Friday Perceval visited a hermit, who turned out to be his uncle. From him the young man learned that the *graal* contained a mass-wafer, and that the Fisher King's invalid father had been kept alive for fifteen years by the daily administration of the sacramental food by the Grail Bearer. Perceval's silence had been caused by his desertion of his mother. Repentant, he stayed with his hermit-uncle over Easter Day in prayer and fasting.

A moment's thought will disclose the inadequacy, even the absurdity, of this explanation. Why did the Grail Bearer use a large platter to hold a single small wafer? Why, since women were forbidden by the Church to administer the sacrament, was she chosen for this office? Since one wafer sufficed to sustain the Fisher King's father, why did she pass through the hall with each course? Why should a question about the father—'Whom does one serve with the Grail?'—effect the cure of the son? The bleeding lance and the second dish, what was their function? What was the causal nexus between Perceval's silence and the desertion of his mother? Who was the monstrous female, and why was she specially concerned with his failure? Surely no admirer of Chrétien's intelligence and art can ascribe to him the invention of this preposterous solution to the mysteries of the Grail. It is the desperate effort of a bungler to find meaning and motivation in a confused traditional story, and presumably Chrétien, though fully conscious of its many weaknesses, meekly took it over from Count Philip's book.

What, then, was the real, the historical, explanation of the traditional story? For over a hundred and fifty years scholars and amateurs have exercised their wits on this problem and have come up with the strangest assortment of answers. In recent times we have been asked to believe that the Grail was derived from the eye of the Egyptian god Thoth, or from a crystal-gazer's ball. Jessie Weston in her all too fascinating book, *From Ritual to Romance*, argued that Grail and lance were sexual symbols, and that the scene in the Grail castle was an initiation rite, which in Christianized form had been brought to Britain. But we have no record of any such ritual; and the cult, if as widespread as Miss Weston thought, would have been denounced by ecclesiastical authorities as heresy. Advocates of Celtic origin have also made their contribution of unsubstantiated guesses, such as the development of the Grail from the cauldron of the Dagda, the Irish Zeus. Not only is a *graal* not a cauldron, but there is no tale told of the Dagda or of his vessel which bears any resemblance to the traditions of the Grail.

To attempt a refutation of the multitudinous mistaken hypotheses and to support with detailed evidence the theory of Celtic origin of the Grail legend is, of course, ruled out by considerations of space. I can merely offer my own interpretation and refer the curious and the sceptical to my book, *The Grail: from Celtic Myth to Christian Symbol*.

If there were any one early Irish or Welsh saga which clearly corresponded to any version of the Grail legend there would be no puzzle, no argument, no wild theorizing, but unfortunately no *immediate* Celtic ancestor of a Grail romance has survived. What we do find, however, scattered through Irish and Welsh literature, are many remnants of the same miscellaneous myths and hero-tales which furnished the material for the quest of the mysterious vessel, and prototypes of the Fisher King, the Grail Bearer, Perceval, and Galahad.

Let us look first at the Welsh contribution. Bran, son of Llyr, who looms so large in the second of the Four Branches of the Mabinogi, was the original of the Maimed King of the Grail romances. Both were distinguished by their lavish hospitality; both were wounded by a javelin in battle. In two French romances the custodian of the Grail bears the name of Bron. There is today a ruinous castle called Dinas Bran, the fortress of Bran, perched on a hill above a salmon river, the Dee. Chrétien and other romancers place the Grail castle beside a river, and represent its lord as a fisher. Bran was the possessor of a miraculous drinking horn, and the Welsh word *corn*, translated in the nominative case into French, gave *cors*; and this was taken to refer to the 'body' of Christ, the Corpus Christi, the miracle-working mass-wafer. Hence the perplexing association of the Grail with the eucharist; hence, too, the name of the Grail castle in the French Vulgate cycle, Corbenic, a scribal error for *cor benoit*, 'blessed horn'. The Grail itself, a capacious platter, which in certain texts provides an abundance of delicious viands, is cousin to the *dysgl* (platter) of Rhydderch: 'whatever food one wished thereon was instantly obtained'.

These might be taken for accidental parallels if it were not for the antecedent probability of Welsh origin and the additional evidence supplied by Irish literature, which, as we know, made its contribution through Wales to the Matter of Britain. One of the most famous of Irish sagas is that of Finn son of Cumal. It was current in Leinster in the eighth century and was still flourishing in the nineteenth throughout Ireland. The *Boyhood Exploits of Finn* tells us that his father was slain in a feud with the sons of Morna. Two women reared the child secretly in the forest, and he grew up to be a skilful hunter with javelins. He took service, unrecognized, with the King of Bantry. He avenged his father's death. He visited his uncle in a desert wood and told him his story. All these features have their counterparts in Chrétien's poem, except the vendetta, and that is found attached to Perceval in the English *Sir Percyvell of Galles*, the French *Prose Tristan* and *Perlesvaus*, and the Welsh *Peredur*.

While the *enfances* of Perceval manifestly derive from the Finn saga, the visit to the Grail castle is a remote cognate of the visit of King Conn to the mansion of the Irish god Lugh, as narrated in a text antedating 1056. The god invites Conn to his abode and arrives before him. A crowned damsel, whom one can identify as the wife of Lugh, provides the guest with huge portions of meat and quantities of ale. The house and Lugh vanish. The same damsel appears in other sagas, as we shall see in Chapter 10, as a monstrous hag, transformed by a kiss into a ravishing beauty. Not only is there a vague correspondence between the saga and Chrétien's poem, but this damsel of the two forms explains what Chrétien failed to explain: who the hideous damsel was who so fiercely upbraided Perceval for his silence at the Grail castle and why she was so concerned. She was the Grail Bearer in another form. Both *Perlesvaus* and *Peredur* support this explanation by identifying the bearer of the platter with the more or less repulsive female who denounced Perceval for his silence. The question test, though not represented in medieval Irish literature, seems to have survived in a folktale collected about a hundred and twenty-five years ago in County Mayo. It has no analogue anywhere else.

Thus the theory of a fusion of Irish myth and heroic legend with similar Welsh material not only supplies prototypes for the chief figures in the Grail legends, and offers parallels to some of the most distinctive narratives, but it also clarifies some of its most tantalizing obscurities. The same hypothesis makes it easier to understand how a writer as brilliant as Chrétien could at times be guilty of such odd lapses in good sense. The blame rests not on his shoulders, but on the inescapable confusions and misunderstandings which a tradition with such a history produced in the course of its long wanderings.

In the last half of the poem the Grail and Perceval are forgotten, and our attention is focused on Gawain. We read of his meeting with a hospitable huntsman king, an amorous affair with that king's sister, a visit to the Castle of Ladies, combined with a nocturnal testing on a perilous bed, more fully described than in *Lancelot*. These are evidently stock motifs which had their origin in Ireland and Wales and which the author of Count Philip's book has patched rather loosely together. Chrétien re-tells them with his usual spirit, but one has a sense that he is a little bewildered as to his purpose. It has been proposed, of late years, that he planned Gawain's adventures as a foil, a contrast, to those of Perceval: Gawain is supposed to be preoccupied with earthly glories and casual amours, whereas Perceval's career is on a loftier plane. But is not this apologia for Chrétien an example of bardolatry, an attempt to convert a fairly obvious defect in the structure of the poem into an artistic virtue? I fail to see that Gawain's affair with the huntsman king's sister is more sensual than Perceval's with Blanchefleur; it certainly did not reach the point of spending the night in bed with her; and Gawain's conduct with the Maid of the Little Sleeves was of exemplary propriety. If this hypothesis be true, and the poet intended a systematic antithesis between the two knights, he bungled the plan badly.

Death must have overtaken him when he was a long way

from completing the stories of Gawain and Perceval, for the poem breaks off abruptly as the former was about to engage in a great duel at a ford. Its unfinished state proved so tempting that four continuations were tacked on to it, which not only added much miscellaneous matter from the storehouse of tradition, but also re-introduced the Grail quest, with new variations. The hero's partial success brings fertility to a Waste Land; he passes a test involving the magical mending of a broken sword; he avenges the murder of his uncle or cousin. The Christianizing process brings about the identification of the bleeding lance with the lance which pierced the side of the crucified Christ, and equates the Grail with a vessel in which Joseph of Arimathea caught the blood which flowed from the wound. Except for the last, these intrusive motifs are best explained as survivals of Irish tradition.

Some scholars have greatly exaggerated the influence of Chrétien on the later Arthurian romances by assuming that he was the inventor of all his stories and arguing that, if a motif, such as the perilous bed or incognito participation in a tournament, is used by a later author, it must have been borrowed from Chrétien. This reasoning is invalidated, of course, by the fact that many of these motifs were included in the repertoire of the *conteurs*. It is also a mistake to argue on the same grounds that the Middle High German *Lanzelet* (*c*.1195) and the Middle English *Sir Percyvell of Galles* (*c*.1330) were based respectively on Chrétien's *Lancelot* and *Perceval*.

Nevertheless, the influence of his five poems was prodigious. They affected the style of many of his French successors. His *Lancelot* was incorporated, with modifications, in the great Vulgate cycle in prose. We have a good abridged version of *Ivain* in Middle English and somewhat free German translations of *Erec* and *Ivain* by Hartmann von Aue. There are also renderings of Chrétien's work in Dutch and Old Norse. In this limited sense, then, it is proper to call him the father of Arthurian romance, but we must not forget what he owed to his progenitors.

WOLFRAM VON ESCHENBACH'S
PARZIVAL

WE HAVE seen how unsatisfactory from a rational and moral point of view was Chrétien's handling of the Grail theme, and how his continuators, far from bringing clarity and sense to its interpretation, made matters worse by the introduction of other traditional matter, such as the hero's obligation to avenge a kinsman's death, or novelties, such as the identification of lance and Grail with relics of the Passion. The *Perceval* presented a challenge. It was accepted by a Bavarian knight and small land-holder, Wolfram von Eschenbach, and by the miracle of genius he created a masterpiece, epic in scope, noble in purpose, humorous, humane, tender, and rational. His *Parzival* has the added interest of being the principal source of Wagner's opera, *Parsifal*.

Wolfram worked on his poem between 1200 and 1210. He alleged as his immediate source a certain Provençal named Kyot, but as no Kyot has been found who qualifies, most critics doubt his existence. On the other hand, it is certain that Books III to XII, and part of Book XIII, are based on Chrétien, Book XIV on the First Continuator. In Book XVI Wolfram speaks deprecatingly of his French predecessor, presumably because he was as bewildered as we are by the treatment of the Grail, by the mystery of the Loathly Damsel, and by other flaws in Chrétien's narrative. Under the pretence of following Kyot, he drastically remodelled and greatly expanded his original. A man of strong religious and moral convictions, he strove to embody them in his poem and to round out the biography of Parzival with an account of his ancestry, of his final achievement of the Grail, of his marriage, his death, and his descendant, the Swan Knight, Loherangrin.

Wolfram's imagination was cramped by the geographic confines of Wales and Logres and he sent his characters far afield. Parzival's father, Gamuret, took military service with the Caliph of Bagdad. His uncle, the hermit Trevrizent, travelled as a young man in the service of love in Asia and Africa, and jousted before Mont Famorgan (Etna) and at Rohaz in modern Jugoslavia. Messengers, sent to seek a cure for the Fisher King's wound, procured herbs which had floated down the rivers of Paradise. Parzival's nephew became the legendary Prester John, a Christian potentate of the Far East.

With intent to enhance the prestige of his hero, Wolfram made his mother the Queen of Waleis and Norgals and his father Gamuret the Angevin, thus suggesting a link with the great Angevin hero of the Third Crusade, Richard the Lion Heart.

Similarly, everything is done to exalt the dignity and power of the Fisher King, Anfortas. Whereas Chrétien surrounded him merely with squires and servants, for Wolfram he is the head of an order of knights called Templeisen and vowed, like the Templars, to celibacy. They are chosen by God Himself and ride out on hazardous missions. Twenty-five ladies of high degree serve the Grail, and as they proceed through the great hall Wolfram stresses their courtly bearing and the drill-like precision of their movements. The Grail Bearer herself was a queen of stainless chastity, clad in silks of Arabia.

Wolfram altered radically Chrétien's concept of the Grail. He did not know, it seems, the meaning of the word *graal*, and his ignorance was shared not only by other translators but even by French miniaturists, who depicted the vessel as a chalice or a covered goblet. He himself mistook the object for a stone; why, no one knows, though there have been numerous guesses. It is no longer a receptacle for the sacramental wafer, even though the magical virtues of the stone, Wolfram later tells us, were derived from such a wafer placed on it every Good

Friday by a dove. The Grail, instead of being carried out of the hall, as in Chrétien, to supply the Fisher King's father with nutriment, is placed before the King himself; and from some source, possibly the First Continuation, Wolfram took over the idea that it served the whole company assembled in the hall with whatever food or drink each man desired. Thus he restored to the Grail the traditional attribute of the Welsh *dysgl* of plenty: 'whatever food one wished thereon was instantly obtained'. Thus he got rid of the anomalous ministration of the eucharist by a woman.

Though we do not know why Wolfram converted the Grail into a stone, it has now been fairly demonstrated what symbolical significance he attached to it. In Book IX the hermit Trevrizent tells Parzival that the name of the stone is '*lapis exilis*'. Scribes miscopied the Latin words in a dozen different ways, and millions of words have been written by the erudite to justify and explain the various corrupt readings. Now Wolfram twice referred to the Grail as '*der wunsch von Pardise*', 'all that one could wish for in the Earthly Paradise', and there is evidence that he had read a famous Latin work, the *Journey of Alexander the Great to Paradise*. There he would have found a *lapis*, described as *exilis* ('small, paltry'). This stone, the size of a human eye, was sent to Alexander from the gate of Paradise to teach him humility and the vanity of worldly glory. Much that has remained obscure about Wolfram's Grail is clarified when one realizes that the stone is—in one aspect at least—a symbol of humility. For humility was one of the virtues which Parzival needed to learn, and it was no accident that Trevrizent, the same teacher who told him the name of the stone, shortly after charged him: 'You must with a meek will guard against pride. . . . Pride has always sunk and fallen. . . . Humility vanquishes pride.' Unfortunately Wolfram failed to make clear the connection between this sage counsel and the symbolic meaning of the stone, and even his contemporaries must have failed to note it, familiar though many of them were with the *Journey of Alexander*.

Nevertheless, they could not miss, any more than we can

today, the poet's sympathetic development of the theme of Parzival's passage from pride to humility—a development to which there is nothing truly comparable in Chrétien. The young knight, triumphant in every contest, welcomed with honour at Arthur's court, a favourite of the ladies, is suddenly subjected to the curses and invectives of the Loathly Damsel, Kundrie. Smarting under the injustice of this public humiliation, Parzival turns in injured pride against God. 'I have devoted myself to His service because I was hopeful of His grace. Now I will forswear His service; if He hates me, I will bear that hatred.' Thus we see that, whereas Chrétien's hero merely drifts aimlessly into alienation from God, Wolfram's Parzival is a declared rebel. For over four years he wanders, nursing his grievance, blaming God for putting him to open shame. Gradually, however, his heart is softened by the tender concern of his female cousin Sigune and by the friendliness of some penitents who remind him that the day is Good Friday, when God proved His love for Man. In chastened mood he meets his hermit uncle, and being instructed by him in the meaning of the Passion, casts off pride and becomes reconciled to God.

Though *Parzival* cannot be considered a philosophical poem, it does take up the perennial problem of God's justice, and I question whether any better theodicy has been propounded by the philosophers than is found in this Arthurian romance.

If Parzival needed to learn humility, he had also to learn compassion; and this theme Wolfram developed with greater clarity, transforming the bewildering question test of Chrétien into a meaningful spiritual experience, a trial of Parzival's feeling for others, his sympathy with suffering. Chrétien at no point intimated that the Fisher King's wound caused him any pain; but Wolfram, while he emphasized the pomp and luxury of the Grail castle, also stressed the agony of its lord, Anfortas. He is no sooner mentioned than we are told that he and joy had parted company. A storm of lamentation broke out when a squire rushed into the hall bearing a spear which streamed with blood—a reminder of some unnamed sorrow. When, after the banquet of the Grail, the King presented Parzival with a sword, he referred to the wound which God had inflicted on him. When the Loathly Damsel, Kundrie, rebuked Parzival, she exclaimed: 'Why, when the sorrowful Fisher sat, reft of joy and comfort, did you not deliver him from his agony? . . . You might have pitied him in his need.' It is in the course of Trevrizent's sermon on pride that the two themes of humility and pity are brought together and intertwined. Speaking of his brother, the Fisher King, the hermit declares:

> 'Sir, there was a king; he was called and is still called Anfortas. You and poor I should ever pity his woe of heart, which was the reward of pride. . . . Only one person has come without bidding to the Grail castle; he was a fool, and he took away with him a sin, because he did not question his host about the pain he saw him bear. . . . He must atone for that sin, that he failed to ask about his host's anguish, which was so keen that no greater was ever known.'

And Parzival presently confesses to his uncle that he was the guilty one: 'Lament my stupidity and lend me true counsel. He who rode up to Munsalvaesche, beheld stark anguish there, and asked no question, was I, wretched boy!' This long interview between Parzival and his uncle is the turning point in the hero's career; for he acknowledges God's love of mankind, learns humility, and the way is prepared for him to show that compassion which will bring the woes of Anfortas to an end.

This occurs in Book XVI. Accompanied by Kundrie and his half-brother Feirefis, Parzival rides up to the Grail castle, and witnesses again the anguish of Anfortas. After praying to the Trinity, he exclaims: 'Mine uncle, what is it afflicts thee?' 'And He who through St Silvester restored a bull to life and Who bade Lazarus arise made Anfortas whole and sound.'

Thus boldly did Wolfram convert the old motif of the question test, so fatuously employed by Chrétien, to point a moral not unlike that of the parable of the Good Samaritan—the virtue of compassion; and it is this moral which Wagner took over and expressed through the *leit-motif*, 'Durch Mitleid wissend, der reine Thor'.

In preaching the virtues of humility and pity, and in demonstrating through Christ's Passion God's love of mankind, the German poet spoke for all medieval Christendom; his is the voice of orthodoxy. But in several striking ways he was not typically medieval. Nowhere in the poem of 24,810 lines is there reference to the cult of the Virgin. There is, on the other hand, an extraordinarily tolerant, even an admiring, attitude towards the heathen. Feirefis, Parzival's half-brother, son of a black queen and himself a worshipper of Jupiter and Juno, is as gallant and magnanimous a knight as any Christian, is at once welcomed into the order of the Round Table, and, after conversion, has no difficulty in winning the Grail Bearer herself as his bride. The heathen queens, Belakane and Secundille, are treated with respect, even though Wolfram does not seem to regard the marriage tie with them as valid. All this sympathy with the heathen evinces an unorthodox, a modern, streak in Wolfram. Strange, too, is the fact that Parzival's confessor, unlike Perceval's, is a layman, and thus, according to strict doctrine, powerless to prescribe penance or offer absolution. For Wolfram God's forgiveness is therefore not dispensed through a priestly intermediary. Celibacy is ordained for the Grail knights, but marriage for their king—evidently an estate at least equal in rank. Though Wolfram was devoutly religious and his outlook is essentially Christian, including submission to God's will, the virtue of meekness, the value of abstinence, the sanctity of marriage, and the sinfulness of amatory adventures, his credo would seem to differ little from that of a 'broad churchman' of today.

To the outstanding features of Wolfram's genius already treated—the wide sweep of his imagination, his bold handling of traditional material, his deep concern with moral problems, his religious liberalism—must be added his consistently ideal-istic attitude towards women. Though he has some caustic comments on the flirts of his acquaintance, he must have known many high-born, great-hearted maids, wives, mothers, and widows who served as models for his characters. He extended his sympathy even to those females whom Chrétien had rendered repellent or malign. The Loathly Damsel who called down curses on Parzival's head Wolfram endowed with a knowledge of languages and science compensating for her monstrous features, and later in the poem she brings Parzival the joyous news of his succession to the kingship and acts as his guide to the Grail castle. Nothing could be more tender and natural than the portrayal of Condwiramurs, Parzival's wife, in whom, we may reasonably conjecture, the poet depicted his own. Her counterpart in Chrétien's *Perceval* was the beautiful but hardly chaste Blanchefleur. Wolfram not only declared that God had bestowed on Condwiramurs every desirable quality, omitting nothing, but he also took pains to remove from her nocturnal visit to Parzival any suspicion of improper motives. When Parzival, after triumphing over her enemies, was obliged to depart, we are assured of their mutual devotion; each found truth in the other. Five years passed during which Parzival dreamed longingly of his wife, but they did not see each other again until, his duty towards his uncle and the Grail kingdom accomplished, he went to meet her. Waked from sleep, she glanced up and saw her husband. She wore nothing but her shift; throwing the coverlet round her, she sprang from her bed to the carpet, and Parzival threw his arms about her. 'I have been told they kissed each other,' says Wolfram—a happy instance of litotes.

In smoothness and charm of style Wolfram is not Chrétien's peer, and he can be charged with naïveté. But his feeling is more fresh, his idealism higher, and for modern readers who are free from fashionable cynicism his story of the Grail quest remains the most intelligible and sympathetic of all medieval versions.

TRISTAN AND ISOLT

WHEN Chrétien drew up in *Erec* a list of the knights of the Round Table, he named among them 'Tristan, who never laughed'; in *Cligès* he asserted his authorship of a poem about King Mark and Isolt the Blonde, which, unluckily, has not survived. As already noted in Chapter 4, Chrétien severely condemned the conduct of Isolt in accepting the embraces of both her husband and her lover, and wrote *Cligès* to show how the situation should be handled. Even earlier, before 1154, the greatest of the troubadours, Bernard de Ventadour, mourning the absence of his mistress, complained that his lot was like that of Tristan without Isolt. Evidently, then, the story of their tragic love was well known in France by the middle of the twelfth century, and for the next three hundred and fifty years it was a favourite subject for artists. In modern times it has been the theme of poets—Tennyson, Swinburne, Arnold, Edwin Arlington Robinson, Hardy, and Masefield. Today literary pilgrims cross the sea to visit the site of the castle which tradition assigned to King Mark, on the cliffs of Tintagel; and Wagner's passionate drama still fills the temples of music.

Whence did this tragic theme whose hero never laughed come? What was its history? Scholars have achieved a large measure of agreement on these questions, but before we concentrate our attention on their results, let us make a brief résumé of the narrative itself, as it is found in the earliest full version, that of the Rhineland poet, Eilhart von Oberge, translated from the French about 1170.

Tristan was the son of Rivalen, lord of Loonois (Lothian

in southern Scotland), and of Blanchefleur, sister of King Mark of Cornwall. His mother died in childbirth, and he was named Tristan because of his father's sorrow. He was trained in all the knightly arts, in manners, and in music; and when he was old enough he sought service with his uncle Mark, but incognito. He and his little company were graciously received. Shortly afterwards, the King of Ireland sent a huge champion, Morold, to claim from Cornwall a tribute of boys and girls; Tristan volunteered to contest the claim, killed Morold, but was himself gravely wounded. He chose to be laid in an open boat with his harp, and was carried by the winds and waves to Ireland, the land of his foes, but it was also the home of Morold's niece, the Princess Isolt, who alone had the skill to cure his poisoned wound. Pretending to be a minstrel who had been attacked by pirates, he escaped recognition, and though he never saw the Princess she supplied healing herbs, and he returned to Cornwall.

A second time he was driven ashore on the Irish coast, this time as the head of a mission to find a bride for his uncle, King Mark. Again he saved himself by a disguise, this time by posing as a merchant with a cargo of food to dispose of. He had a bit of luck, too, for a dragon was opportunely devastating the country, and the Princess Isolt was offered as a bride to whoever destroyed the monster. Alone, Tristan performed the feat, and cut out the tongue as proof, but fell unconscious from the burns he had suffered. The King of Ireland's seneschal—seneschals usually played the villain's role in medieval fiction because minstrels as a class were at war with them—found the dragon's carcass, cut off the head, and came back to the court to claim Isolt's hand. She, however, knew better than to believe him, found the unconscious Tristan, and revived him. While he was taking a bath she happened to pick up his sword and spied a breach in it which proved that he was the slayer of her uncle Morold. She swore revenge, but her maid Brangien added to Tristan's entreaties the argument that if she killed him she condemned herself to marriage with the pretender. So she relented; Tristan produced the dragon's tongue and proved his claim to her hand, but, faithful to his uncle, he renounced it in King Mark's favour.

On the voyage to Cornwall, as everyone knows, Tristan and Isolt drank the fateful potion which had been intended for Mark and his bride. No longer free of will, they were bound in the chains of love for four years. Mark wedded the Irish princess, but was deceived in the bridal bed by the substitution of Brangien for the Queen. Fearful, as a consequence, that Brangien would betray the secret, Isolt bribed two knights to murder her, but the plot failed and she repented of her treachery. Once, when she came to a tryst with her lover beneath a linden, she saw the figure of Mark spying on them from its branches, and by affecting indignation with Tristan persuaded Mark of her innocence. On another occasion, the lovers were less fortunate; Mark ordered Tristan to be broken on the wheel and Isolt to be burned, but was persuaded by some lepers to give her to them to satisfy their lusts. Tristan, managing to escape, rescued her, and fled with her to a forest. Here, though they led a hard life, they found bliss in their love. Once Mark was led to their refuge, and when he found them sleeping with a sword between them he was again convinced that they were guiltless and spared them.

At the end of four years, according to Eilhart's version, the effect of the philtre abated and the lovers now found their hardships intolerable. Professing repentance for his sin, Tristan persuaded a hermit to intercede for them with the King, but though Mark consented to receive back his wife, he banished her lover. We next read of Tristan's knightly exploits in the service of the King of Gavoie (Galloway), and then at Arthur's court, where he was welcomed by Gawain especially. He joined a hunting party which, by Gawain's contrivance, sought hospitality at Mark's castle in order that Tristan might see his mistress. When at night he seized the opportunity to visit her bed he cut himself on blades set about it, and so left evidence of his guilt. But Gawain was equal to the situation; all the guests out of loyalty to Tristan proceeded to cut themselves on the blades, so that the guilt could not be pinned on the culprit.

Leaving Britain, Tristan came to Carhaix in Brittany; there he delivered King Hoel from his enemies and won the friendship of his son, Kaherdin. When told that Kaherdin's sister bore the name Isolt he consented to marry her, but left her a virgin. As she rode with her brother across a pool, some water splashed up under her dress to her knee, and she remarked that no man had been so bold. Kaherdin, thus learning her secret, reproached Tristan with the slight he had put on her and her family. Tristan justified himself by asserting that he had a mistress more beautiful and loving than his wife, and offered to prove it. So, crossing the sea to Cornwall, the two friends watched by the side of the road while a hunting party passed by, ending with the Queen's waiting women and the Queen herself. Admitting that even the handmaids surpassed his sister in beauty, Kaherdin became reconciled to Tristan.

A false report reached Isolt that her lover, when pursued by King Mark's men, had failed to turn and face them, although conjured to do so in her name. She was deeply incensed, and when he sought to plead his innocence, disguised as a leper, she had him driven away with blows. Angry in his turn, he sought solace by consummating his marriage with his wife. In a few months Isolt the Queen was overcome with remorse for her cruelty and as a penance wore a hair shirt night and day. When a messenger brought news of this to Tristan, and implored him in Isolt's name to forget his wrongs, he could not but consent, and thus the lovers were reconciled. There follow three episodes in which Tristan adopted the disguises of a pilgrim, a minstrel, and a jester and contrived to meet and lie with his mistress. Returned to Cornwall, he accompanied Kaherdin to an assignation; Kaherdin was killed by the lady's husband, and Tristan was wounded so sorely that the leeches could do nothing for him. Only Isolt the Queen could cure him.

He sent a merchant to her with a token ring, to beseech

her aid, and bidding him raise a white sail on his return if she were with him; a black if she were not. Thus summoned, the Queen left all and fled with the merchant. Tristan's wife learned the secret of the sails, and when the vessel approached bearing her rival she told Tristan that the sail was black. The lie killed Tristan, and instantly she repented it. Let me translate.

Then, when the Queen disembarked and heard the great lamentation, her sorrow was heavy. 'Alas!' she said, 'woe is me! Tristan is dead!' But she turned neither red nor pale, nor did she weep any more, though in her heart was great anguish. Hear now what she did. Silently she went to the chamber where the knight lay on his bier. Close by stood his wife, weeping and wailing sorely. The Queen said to her: 'Lady, thou shouldst stand aside and let me come nearer. I have better cause to mourn than thou; that mayest thou well believe. He was dearer to me than ever he was to thee.' She turned back the covering that was on the bier, and pushed Tristan's body a little farther over. Then she sat down by the knight, and spoke never a word more, but laid herself close beside him and died.

This is the favourite love-story of the Middle Ages in its crudest form. There are gross inconsistencies. Mark at one point is so despicable that he is willing to deliver his wife into the hands of lepers to satisfy their lust, but at the end he is forgiving and magnanimous to a degree which few cuckolds attain. The lovers, judged by the Christian and the feudal codes, are guilty of the most serious offences. Tristan is a bounder, faithless to his uncle and his king. Isolt is a hardened vixen, who attempts the murder of her too faithful handmaid, and who brazens out her adultery year after year. According to certain versions, she even mocks God Himself by taking an equivocal oath on holy relics which enables her to pass the ordeal of red-hot iron unscathed. And the reader's sympathies are always engaged on the side of the sinners. Yet it should be noted that the author, at least, regarded the compulsive power of the philtre as a valid extenuation of their conduct, and, though he catered to popular interest in illicit love, he did not indulge in pornographic detail. And there is a touch of romantic idealism in the notion that a lover must grant any request made in his lady's name.

The artistic and moral crudities of Eilhart's narrative are the consequences of its previous history. The researches of the last seventy years have shown that the romance of Tristan and Isolt is, like the traditions about Arthur, a conglomeration of many elements about a single historic figure, and have made it possible to follow the process of development with remarkable precision.

Its origin lies in the land of the Picts, who occupied most of Scotland north of the Firths of Clyde and Forth, until they were conquered by and amalgamated with the Scots, colonists from Ireland. There were a number of Pictish kings named Drust or Drustan, and one of them, who reigned briefly about 780, was the son of Talorc. It can hardly be a coincidence that when Trystan or Drystan appears in Welsh literature he is always the son of Tallwch; and the possibility is eliminated when it is realized that Drust became by the tenth century the hero of a version of the Perseus and Andromeda legend which influenced surely some of the earlier incidents in Tristan's career. According to Drust's legend, he arrived at a fort on one of the Hebrides, islands which lay west of Pictland. He heard sounds of lament and learned that the daughter of the King of the Isles was shortly to be delivered as tribute to three giants. Drust defeated the giants and rescued the Princess, but was wounded. He must have worn a helmet covering his face, for, though the Princess bound up his wound, she could not recognize him as her rescuer by his features. But her father commanded all those who claimed credit for her deliverance to take a bath in her presence, and she detected Drust by the bandage. The false claimants were discomfited, and the King of the Isles offered Drust his daughter in wedlock, but he refused. Here it is easy to distinguish the

source of Tristan's arrival at the court of Mark, the lamentation over the tribute, the victory over Morold, the wound, the
false claimants to the slaying of the dragon, the recognition of
Tristan in the bath by the Princess Isolt, Tristan's refusal of
her hand. The little romance of Drust is the nucleus of the
long romance of Tristan.

The northern origin is probably preserved in the fact that
Tristan's birthplace in Eilhart and the French texts is usually
Loonois or Loenois, and that undoubtedly means the district
of Lothian, which, though not included in Pictland, bordered
it on the south. The name of the forest to which the lovers
were banished is Morois, and it is a fair surmise that it refers
to the wild district of Moray in northern Scotland.

The Pictish saga of Drust must have passed by way of the
Britons of Strathclyde to the Welsh, and here in Wales we find
Drystan son of Tallwch linked with Esyllt and March son of
Meirchiawn, the Isolt and the Mark of the French romances.
A love-story about these three characters, of which the original
tale of Drust knew nothing, has been added, and it has been
shown conclusively that it was patterned after the famous Irish
saga, the *Elopement of Diarmaid and Grainne*, of which there are
fragments as early as the tenth century, though the complete
text is late. Diarmaid, like Tristan, was beloved by his uncle's
wife, violated the obligations of friendship and loyalty, and
fled with her to the forest. At first, he did not cohabit with her,
and placed a stone between them each night—a practice
which evidently accounts for the otherwise senseless presence
of a sword between Tristan and Isolt as they lay side by side.
Perhaps the most striking parallel is the occurrence in both the
saga and the romance of the episode of the splashing water;
Grainne, as well as Isolt of Brittany, remarked on the boldness
of the water as compared with the restraint of the man. To
clinch the matter, a Welsh text of the sixteenth century tells
a story of Trystan and Esyllt and March which exactly corresponds to the Irish saga of Diarmaid and Grainne and Finn. It
was Ireland, then, which contributed the central theme of
adulterous love to the tragic romance of Tristan.

From Wales the legend seems to have followed the usual route of Arthurian traditions to Cornwall and Brittany. Presumably Cornish raconteurs with a right instinct fixed on the headland of Tintagel as an appropriate setting for the romantic story; and ever since the crumbling walls of the castle, the chasm, and the little cove have been associated with the star-crossed lovers. Recent scholarship, to be sure, has discovered an alternative residence of King Mark at Lantyan near Fowey, but Tennyson and Swinburne have made it impossible to associate Tristan and Isolt with any other place than Tintagel, where the Atlantic billows beat against the cliffs.

The first sign that the conglomerate story of adulterous passion had crossed the Channel to the Continent is the name of a certain Tristan who inherited the barony of Vitré near Rennes in 1030. There can be little doubt that he was so christened because the story had achieved a vogue in Brittany by the year 1000. The history of Tristan of Vitré seems to have influenced in turn the growing legend, for his father's name, Rivalen, replaced the Tallwch of Welsh tradition, and his wars with the Duke of Brittany seem to be reflected in certain versions of the romance. The pathetic tale of Rivalen's love for King Mark's sister Blanchefleur and of her death in child-bed was probably composed by Bretons who naturally assumed that her child was named Tristan because of the sad (French *triste*) circumstances of his birth. This unhappy connotation of the name surely tended to give a dark colouring to his later history also.

We may attribute to the Bretons, in fact, most of the episodes beginning with his services to King Hoel and his fateful marriage to the second Isolt and ending with the superb death scene. But the complex of incidents involving Tristan, his bride, and her brother was not pure invention, for in essentials it was derived from the love-story, famous throughout the Moslem world, of the poet Kais (who died a hundred years before the Pictish Drust) and his wife Lobna. Like Tristan, Kais was forced to leave the lady with whom he was linked in undying affection; like Tristan, he met another woman bearing the same name, and with her brother's encouragement married her; like Tristan he would not consummate the marriage and thereby offended her family; according to one version Kais, like Tristan, was buried in the same grave with his love. How this Arabic romance of deathless love came to the knowledge of the man who provided it with a Breton setting and Breton characters, no one can say, but it was probably through the highly civilized Moors of southern Spain.

It was a genius, surely, perhaps this same man, who composed the tragic finale. In it we hear echoes of old Greek romance. The message which the dying lover sends to his mistress imploring her to come and heal his poisoned wound as she alone could do, his death in the belief she had failed him, and her arrival too late—these must have been suggested by the poignant tale of Paris and Oenone. As for the motif of the black and white sails, we may seek its origin either in the classical story of the death of Aegeus, or in a folktale which was still current in the islands off the Breton coast less than a hundred years ago.

As Bédier perceived, the Tristan romance is a composite to which Picts, Welsh, Cornish, and Bretons made their contributions. Though assuming in the later stages of its development a grandeur of design, it is nevertheless a patchwork of the comic and the tragic, the savage and the civilized, the cynical and the idealistic. In somewhat the same form as it reached the composer of Eilhart's source, it reached other French and Anglo-Norman poets of the second half of the twelfth century, who recognized its fascination and power. We know the names of some of them—Chrétien de Troyes, Li Kievre, Marie de France, Béroul, and Thomas. The poems of Chrétien and Li Kievre are lost, and that of Marie, the *Lai of the Honeysuckle*, deals only with a single episode: the arrangement of an assignation by means of a message cut by Tristan on a hazel wand and placed by him on the road where Queen Isolt was to pass.

The *Tristan* of Béroul, though often attributed to a single poet of that name, has recently been shown to embody the work of two poets. It is a fragment of 4485 lines, lacking a beginning and an end. Béroul himself wrote 2765 lines, and seems to have used a source, the *estoire*, which Eilhart also followed. But with line 2766 the anonymous continuator not only abandoned the narrative pattern of Eilhart but also introduced violent contradictions of his predecessor and exhibited some idiosyncrasies of style and versification. There is no clue to the date of the first part, but an allusion to the epidemic which struck the Crusaders at Acre seems to date the second part after 1191.

Nevertheless, there are similarities between them. Both authors used the Norman dialect; both intended their work to be read aloud since there are frequent addresses to a listening audience. They were both masters of dialogue and descriptive detail. It is not easy to forget the scene where Mark, learning from a forester that he had seen Tristan and Isolt sleeping under a shelter of branches in the Forest of Morois, set out to wreak vengeance; nor how, when he found them clothed, with a sword lying between them, he placed his glove, in a revulsion of pity, so that the sun would not shine in Isolt's eyes, and substituted his own sword for his nephew's as a token of reconciliation and trust.

But this exhibition of generous feeling seems out of place in a poem where moral scruples are forgotten, no one trusts anyone else for long, and even the lovers cease temporarily to love. The effect of the potion wears off after three years, Tristan and Isolt tire of the life together in the forest, and feel a transient twinge of repentance. But, having returned on the advice of an easy-going hermit to King Mark, Isolt becomes more than ever before the accomplished deceiver. Arranging with her paramour to meet her in a leper's disguise at a muddy ford, she mounts on his back while he carries her across in view of all the courtiers of Mark and King Arthur. Thus the next day she swears by God and all the holy relics that never has any man entered between her thighs except the leper and her lawful spouse. She succeeds in convincing the world that she is innocent, and we, the readers, are expected to admire her cleverness. There is no word of censure.

But there must have been many who, though fascinated by the dramatic element in the tradition, could not stomach the crudities and the complete immorality. Perceiving, perhaps, the idealistic element introduced by the story of Kais and Lobna, and influenced doubtless by the cult of sublimated, non-marital love expressed in the lyrics of the troubadours, a poet named Thomas composed a somewhat drastic revision of the story.

Only fragments of his poem have survived, but with the aid of redactions we can reconstruct its narrative content. He twice denies any experience in affairs of love, and this, combined with several typical attacks on the fair sex, points to one who had taken at least the minor orders and was vowed to celibacy. There are slight Anglo-Norman features in the texts, and there is an encomium on London as a city unsurpassed in Christendom; so it seems that, although he may have been born elsewhere, he at least lived for a considerable time in England. It has often been urged that he wrote for Eleanor of Aquitaine, Queen of England, who was both a patroness of literature and, by reputation at least, an advocate of the freer and more idealistic concepts of love which the troubadours proclaimed. But is it probable that anyone seeking to recommend himself to a woman would have repeatedly denounced womankind? Some heraldic evidence, though indecisive, hints that Thomas wrote rather for her husband, Henry II, or one of his sons, and perhaps as late as 1185.

The Tristan legend came to him in a form not unlike that which we find in Eilhart. It is hardly an accident that he invoked the authority of Breri, that is, Bleheris, and that Eilhart named a minor character Pleherin. He retained some of the most shocking features of the old story—Isolt's plot to murder Brangien and her equivocal oath. But he expunged Mark's surrender of Isolt to the lustful embraces of the lepers, and for the most part he treated the royal cuckold with respect and sympathy.

The most drastic changes which Thomas made concern the life of Tristan and Isolt in the forest and their return. Whereas Eilhart and Béroul had depicted the lovers as miserable and at last disillusioned and repentant, not so Thomas. He represents their banishment as an idyllic interlude; and he will allow no abatement of the spell imposed by the philtre. Great love must be lasting. Two long passages of soliloquy, such as Chrétien introduced in *Cligès*, reveal the ebb and flow of Tristan's feelings as he is torn between a physical attraction to his wife, Isolt of Brittany, and a passionate loyalty to Isolt the Queen. The situation may be fanciful—that a man should marry a woman merely because of her name—but the psychological conflict is handled with realism and power. The poet's clerical calling does not lead him to minimize the depth, faith, and endurance of this unhallowed love; and he loses all prolixity as he describes Isolt the Queen landing in Brittany, hastening up the steep street, lifting her long gown before her, the wonder of the people at her beauty, the tolling of the bells, and the last despairing words over Tristan's body. The poem closes with a moving epilogue:

> Here Thomas ends his book. He gives greeting to all lovers, the grave and the amorous, the jealous and the desirous, the happy and the despairing, to all those who will hear these verses. If I have not pleased all in what I have said, I have done the best after my skill. . . . I have written this to give an example and to render the story more beautiful so that it may please lovers, and that, here and there, they may find somewhat to remember and that they may have great solace from it, despite change, despite wrong, despite pain, despite grief, despite all the wiles of love.

Thomas's poem enjoyed a considerable prestige, especially in England and northern Europe. A series of tile designs based on it were laid down as flooring in the monasteries of Chertsey and Hales Owen. A monk made a faithful though abridged translation in 1226 for King Haakon of Norway, the *Tristrams-saga*. These facts suggest a remarkable tolerance on the part of the pious for this epic of adultery, which might at a later date have been on the Index Expurgatorius. Two explanations are possible: plain laxity, which was certainly prevalent enough in the Middle Ages, or the excuse that Tristan and Isolt had not really sinned against God and Man because the potion had taken away their power of will. In fact, an Italian romance, the *Tavola Ritonda*, reported as a rumour that Pope Agapitus, learning that enchantment and not evil intent was responsible for the amour, granted indulgence from penance to all who prayed for the souls of the lovers.

By great good luck the Anglo-Norman *Tristan* came into the hands of a more accomplished poet, a more original thinker, and a greater idealist than Thomas, Gottfried von Strassburg. Neither a knight nor an ecclesiastic, he must have belonged to the upper circle of highly literate laity in the flourishing Alsatian city, at a time when all Germany and Austria were thrilled by the discovery of French romance and Provençal lyric. He was widely read in Latin, French, and German literature, not only in belles-lettres, but also in mystical theology, law, and rhetoric. A contemporary and a caustic critic of Wolfram, he wrote his *Tristan* about 1210, but for some unknown reason left it incomplete, breaking off before the marriage of his hero to Isolt of Brittany.

As an artist, Gottfried displayed a remarkable virtuosity in word-play and verbal music, sometimes at the expense of clarity of thought; and this charm of style is lost, of course, on those who can read him only in translation. But his greatest gifts lay in the depth of his feeling and the subtlety of his thinking, which raise him above the level even of Thomas.

As a thinker, he saw in the tragic legend, vividly set forth, the opposition between the *mariage de convenance*, on the one hand, so firmly established in feudal and bourgeois society and sanctioned by the Church, and, on the other hand, the union of hearts. He would not, as Chrétien did in *Cligès*, offer an un-realistic method of escape to lovers by means of a sleeping

potion. He faced the hard facts, and drew the logical consequence that for noble spirits suffering was inseparable from
love, was indeed a condition of true loving. 'He who has never
experienced the pangs of love has never known its joy.'

Gottfried seems also to concede that in this harsh world
love out of wedlock involves deceit, disloyalty, and even worse
crimes. By a supreme irony, *Minne*, which is the spring of all
the loftiest qualities in man and woman, also forces them to
violate the moral and the Christian code. In terms of the story,
the love-philtre was a compulsive force, which, while it inspired in Tristan and Isolt the most gracious and generous
feelings, and conferred on them moments of exquisite bliss,
compelled them to sin and to suffer. It was society, however,
which was the real villain, which was responsible for the sin
and suffering—society with its political marriages, its cruel
ordinances, its cold neglect of the claims of the heart.

Gottfried was in hearty sympathy with the idealistic strain
in the romance which was absorbed from the troubadours and
the author of Kais and Lobna—the concept of love as an
overmastering, lasting, ennobling passion, and the source of
supreme joy. It is when the lovers are detached from society,
apart from its petty concerns and brutal constrictions, that the
ideal existence is possible. And Gottfried took the opportunity
offered by Thomas's idyllic description of the life in the forest
to express his concept of what love in its perfection could mean.
Let me quote from Jessie Weston's beautiful, somewhat free
translation:

> Many have marvelled wherewith the twain might
> support their life in the wilderness, but in truth they needed
> little save each other, the true love and faith they bare the
> one to the other. . . . Nor did it vex them that they were
> thus alone in the wild woodland: what should they want
> with other company? They were there together; a third
> would have made unequal what was equal, and oppressed
> that fellowship that was so fair. Even good King Arthur
> never had at his court a feast that might have brought them

greater joy and refreshment. . . . They had a court, they had a council, which brought them nought but joy. Their courtiers were the green trees, the shade and the sunlight, the streamlet and the spring; flowers, grass, leaf and blossom, which refreshed their eyes. Their service was the song of the birds, the little brown nightingales, the throstles and the merles, and other wood-birds. The siskin and the ring-dove vied with each other to do them pleasure; all day long their music rejoiced ear and soul. Their love was their high feast, which brought them a thousand times daily the joy of Arthur's Round Table and the fellowship of his knights. What might they ask better? The man was with the woman, and the woman with the man; they had the fellowship they most desired, and were where they fain would be. . . .

The glade was their pleasure-ground; they wandered hither and thither, hearkening each other's speech and waking the song of the birds by their footsteps. . . . When the sun grew high in the heavens, they betook themselves to the linden; its branches offered them a welcome shelter, the breezes were sweet and soft beneath its shade, and the couch at its feet was decked with the fairest grass and flowers. There they sat side by side, those true lovers, and told each other tales of those who ere their time had suffered and died for love. . . . But when they would think of them no more, they turned them again to their grotto and took the harp, and each in turn sang to it softly lays of love and of longing; now would Tristan strike the harp while Isolt sang the words, then it would be the turn of Isolt to make music while Tristan's voice followed the notes. Full well might it be called the Love Grotto.

This same grotto was a temple consecrated to the virtues inspired by love but so difficult to practise in the outer world. The roundness represented singleness of heart, without cunning or treachery; the breadth signified love's boundless power; the height, the aspiring heart; the white wall, spotless rectitude;

and the marble floor, unshaken stability. The light of good repute shone through the three windows of kindness, humility, and noble manners. In the midst was the bed of symbolic crystal, dedicated to the goddess Minne. She and no other divinity presided over this temple of sublimated passion.

It is evident that the poet is applying to this essentially non-Christian shrine the symbolic method of interpretation which pious authors applied to the architecture of the Christian church—the apse, the transepts, the doors, and so forth. In similar fashion Gottfried employed the terminology of religious mysticism, and even some of its imagery, in setting forth his theories of human love. Of his own poem he wrote: 'This is bread for all noble hearts; with this the death of both lives on. We read of their life, we read of their death, and it is to us as sweet as bread.' Though not a parody, this is at least a bold misappropriation of the doctrine of the bread of life, the eucharist. Note, too, that Gottfried invoked Apollo and the Muses and not the Holy Spirit. He recognized God, to be sure, and gave Him credit for never forgetting noble hearts, and for Tristan's victory over Morolt. All this, however, sounds rather conventional. God did not seem particularly mindful of the welfare, spiritual or otherwise, of those noble hearts, Tristan and Isolt. And what is one to make of the notorious comment which Gottfried made on the success of Isolt's equivocal oath? By large gifts of jewels, palfreys, and so forth, to charity, we are told, she sought to ingratiate herself with the Deity, so that He would turn a blind eye to her guilt. Apparently, the oath being ambiguous, the divine clemency accepted it as truth, and permitted her to carry the red-hot iron unscathed. Gottfried remarks:

> Thus it was shown and proved to all the world that the most virtuous Christ is blown about like a sleeve in the wind. . . . He is at the disposition of every heart, for honourable purposes or dishonourable. Whether it is a matter of deadly earnest or a light affair, He accommodates Himself to what you wish.

Some critics think that this is not blasphemous and heretical but merely a sardonic reflection on the fallibility of the ordeal by red-hot iron, which as a matter of fact had become so discredited that in 1215 the Church itself refused to recognize its validity. But when one considers the poem as a whole, which without doubt finds the source of goodness and the highest ecstasy, not in the love of God, but in the love of woman, of a mistress, how can one reconcile these sentiments with orthodoxy? Moreover, it must be realized that Gottfried lived in the same world and was subject to the same influences as Walther von der Vogelweide, the greatest of medieval German lyric poets, who wrote: 'Who says that love is sin, let him consider well. Many an honour dwells with her, and troth and happiness.' 'He happy man, she happy woman, whose hearts are to each other true; both lives increased in price and worth; blessed their years and all their days.' Is all this reconcilable with the teaching of the Church? Listen to Honorius of Autun: 'Nothing so estranges Man from God as the love of women.'

If one may judge by the number of illustrations in the visual arts of painting, sculpture, and embroidery, the romance of Tristan and Isolt, even in the degenerate form of the French prose version and its progeny, was by far the most popular secular story of the Middle Ages. Most of the Arthurian romances, however, do not end in tragedy, but, whatever the reason, in lovers' meeting and eventually wedding. A typical example is that of Sir Gareth of Orkney and Dame Lyones in Malory. Apparently, though the love-match may have been exceptional, it was regarded as the ideal. And when Chaucer came to write towards the end of the fourteenth century and ran through the gamut of sexual experience in the *Canterbury Tales*, he set down the mature results of his reflection on the subject in the Franklin's Tale.

> Love wol nat be constrained by maistrye. . .
> Love is a thing as any spirit free;
> Wommen of kinde [by nature] desiren libertee,
> And not to been constrained as a thral. . .

Here may men seen an humble wis accord:
Thus hath she take hir servant and hir lord—
Servant in love and lord in mariage. . .
Who coude tell but he had wedded be
The joy, the ese, and the prosperitee
That is bitwix an housbond and his wif?

THE VULGATE CYCLE

THE great conflict between the idealization of adultery and the institution of marriage and the additional conflict between both of these and the cult of virginity and celibacy preached by the Church are illustrated more fully than elsewhere, though not more lucidly, in that enormous library of Arthurian fiction called, because of its popularity with the reading public, the Vulgate cycle. One book, the *Lancelot*, is a frank glorification of idealized adultery; another book, the *Mort Artu*, though sympathetic to the lovers, is a condemnation of adultery; the *History of the Holy Grail*[1] and the *Quest of the Holy Grail* exalt the celibate ideal, and their authors would doubtless echo the pronouncement of Honorius of Autun. It is somewhat as if Byron's *Don Juan* had been continued by Thomas Hardy and completed by Charles Williams. Of course, the inconsistencies are numerous, the main themes are obscured by totally irrelevant matter, the workmanship is very uneven. Yet it is an amazing fact that, viewed in the large, this conglomeration of material was finally revised and moulded to form a majestic structure. To it, indeed, Sir Thomas Malory owed, more or less directly, much that is best in the design of his masterpiece. For, though starting out as a romance of sublimated adultery, it gradually reveals how such a passion may not only close the road to spiritual development but also, by violating the bonds of marriage, friendship, and feudal loyalty, bring about the downfall of a kingdom and the wreck of a noble fellowship.

One would expect that in a corpus so vast—the edition consists of some twelve hundred folio pages—there would be

[1] Not to be confused with *Perlesvaus*, translated by Sebastian Evans as the *High History of the Holy Grail*.

found reliable clues as to the authors. But, on the contrary, the attribution in the manuscripts of certain parts of the work to Walter Map, a Norman-Welsh clerk in the household of King Henry II, is now generally rejected, whereas the claim of the *History of the Holy Grail* to be a transcript from a book penned by Christ's own hand is even less credible. One may assume that all the authors of the cycle were tonsured, and the little evidence we have suggests that they lived and wrote in Champagne or Burgundy between 1210 and 1230. Not unnaturally, being Frenchmen, they converted Lancelot du Lac, whose antecedents we have detected in the Welsh Lluch Llauynnauc, into a French prince.

The first book of the cycle to be composed, frequently called the *Prose Lancelot*, tells at great length and with many divagations the story of his early years and of his passion for Guenevere. His father was Ban, King of Benoic, an imaginary country in western France. Immediately after Ban's tragic death, a fay snatched up his infant son and plunged with him into a lake, and his grief-stricken widow retired to a nunnery. Though it was from this lake that the infant came to be called Lancelot du Lac, the author, being a realist, informs us that it was merely an illusion created by the fairy to hide her palace; and there she brought up her precocious foster-child until at the age of eighteen he was not only a paragon of manly beauty but also an adept in sports and a model of courtly behaviour. Then, learning of his ardent wish to seek knighthood at Arthur's court, she was deeply distressed but nevertheless equipped him with horse and arms, and gave him a long sociological discourse on the origins of knighthood and the duty of knights to maintain justice, punish evil-doers, and, above all, to protect the Holy Church. A very churchly fairy!

She conducted him to Britain, introduced him to Arthur, with the request that he be promptly knighted, and departed. Events followed fast. Lancelot fell in love with Guenevere at first sight. As soon as he had received the accolade, he undertook two most dangerous exploits. When, bashfully, he asked the Queen whether he might be her knight, and she replied with the conventional but tantalizingly ambiguous words 'God be with you, fair sweet friend [*ami*]', the young man's fate was sealed. He deliberately contrived to obtain his sword from the Queen, thus dividing his allegiance, as it were, between the King who had dubbed him and the Queen who had accepted him as her knight. Suffering in secret, he displayed the conventional symptoms of his malady, but meanwhile carried out the most prodigious feats of arms. With the aid of magic shields sent him by the Lady of the Lake he accomplished the conquest of the Dolorous Garde, and there on a tomb read what he had not known before, his name and parentage. Thenceforth the castle was called Joyous Garde.

A new and important figure enters the story, Galehot, lord of the Faraway Isles, Malory's Galahault the Haut Prince, Dante's Galeotto. The story of his friendship for Lancelot, his aiding the bashful knight's suit, and his premature death forms one of the most artistic and moving parts of the Vulgate cycle. He invades Britain with a hundred thousand horsemen, and would have overcome Arthur but for his great magnanimity and his utter admiration for Lancelot, who is fighting incognito on Arthur's side. At Lancelot's request he goes so far as to surrender himself to Arthur. Remaining at court, he learns of the Queen's interest in the unknown knight who has brought peace to the land, and whose identity with Lancelot she has begun to suspect. So he arranges the assignation made famous by Dante's allusion to Galeotto as a go-between. Guenevere, attended by two of her ladies, meets with Lancelot, attended by Galehot and a seneschal, at dusk in a meadow. The Queen takes the initiative with her pale and trembling lover, questions him as to his identity, and elicits from him the confession that ever since she had addressed him ambiguously as 'fair sweet friend' he had considered himself altogether hers. At Galehot's urging she takes pity on him, raises his chin with her hand, and gives him a long kiss. Then she, in turn, declares herself to be wholly his. The moon has risen before the group leaves the meadow.

Other trysts followed, but it was only when, long

afterwards, Arthur himself was false to his marriage vows that Lancelot and Guevenere consummated their love. Thus, evidently, the author sought to excuse their adultery by imputing to Arthur the same offence. He also stressed the nobility of Galehot, who with utter unselfishness promoted an affair that tended to separate him from his friend. Galehot becomes a tragic figure, doomed to see his castles fall in ruins, and destined to starve himself to death in the anguished belief that Lancelot was dead.

In sharp contrast to Lancelot, the ideal lover, and to Galehot, the perfect friend, stands Arthur. It is true that Chrétien had already degraded him in two of his poems, but in the *Prose Lancelot* the King is progressively belittled and besmirched. Lust leads him into a trap set by a Saxon enchantress, and to what lower depths could the legendary champion of the Britons descend? He is duped into believing that Guenevere is an impostor, banishes her, and lives for two and a half years with a false Guenevere. Was it French hatred of England, kindled by the wars between the two countries leading up to the battle of Bouvines (1214), that was responsible for this libellous portrayal of Arthur?

The interrelations between Lancelot, Guenevere, and Galehot are much more complicated than the few paragraphs here devoted to them would indicate. Moreover, the complexity of the narrative is deliberately increased by the adoption of the technique called 'interlacing'. Any long novel with many characters may turn from the main set of characters to another, and then to still another, before returning to the original group; but, if the novel possesses any measure of coherence, the actions of these several groups and individuals affect each other. It is a serious flaw in the structure of the *Prose Lancelot* that many episodes are totally irrelevant to the main theme or themes. Monotony is another defect: three times Lancelot is imprisoned by Morgan le Fay and spurns her amorous advances; three times he goes raving mad for one cause or another. Sometimes the motivation is childish or implausible. Apart from the idealized treatment of love and friendship already discussed, the moral tone is rather low. Even Gawain and his brother Gurrehes behave in a fashion which reflects little credit on the practical ethics of the Round Table.

Interspersed, however, through this largely amoral book are passages, long or short, which reflect a distinctly pious personality. It was he, perhaps, who assigned to the Lady of the Lake the sermon on the duties of knighthood, with special emphasis on the protection of the Church. We may recognize his handiwork in the speech of the wise clerk Helyes predicting that the high adventure of the Grail will never be achieved by Lancelot on account of his sin, but by a knight of stainless chastity. These and similar interpolations give the *Prose Lancelot* its curiously ambivalent tone; they also show that whoever made them, though probably not the composer of the *Quest of the Holy Grail* or the *Mort Artu*, was involved in the grandiose plan to link up the three books and knew the general nature of what was to follow the *Lancelot*.

More than that, it seems that this same pious interpolator undertook the task of connecting the predominantly worldly romance of *Lancelot* with the consistently religious allegory of the *Quest* by making the sinning hero of the one the father of Galahad, the saintly hero of the other. This device is regarded by some distinguished scholars, not as the late inspiration of an interpolator, but as the germinal idea out of which the Vulgate cycle developed. It has also been acclaimed as a brilliant invention, without any basis in antecedent tradition. With all due respect to those who hold these views, I venture to question them. There is good, though not conclusive, evidence that before Lancelot was established by Chrétien as the unalterably faithful lover of Guenevere, a legend was in circulation to the effect that he had begotten out of wedlock a son named Galaain or Galvain, who was destined to equal or surpass his father.

It is not certain, therefore, that this method of linking the *Lancelot* to the *Quest* originated with one of the authors of the composite work. It is even more doubtful that the device, whether traditional or invented, was a felicitous one. Some readers, at least, must feel that the story of the begetting of Galahad as told in the *Lancelot* or in Malory's modified version verges on the absurd and the repulsive.

When Lancelot came by chance to Corbenic, the Grail castle, he proved himself superior to all other knights; first, by lifting a maiden out of a scalding bath in which she had sat for several winters, and, secondly, by opening a tomb and killing a fire-breathing dragon. Recognized by these feats, he was hailed by King Pelles, lord of the castle, as one whose progeny was destined to deliver the land from strange adventures. That evening a dove flew into the hall with a censer in its mouth, filling the air with incense. All present knelt in prayer. The King's beautiful daughter entered, bearing a very rich chalice, and as she passed along the tables they were filled with delicious viands. She departed, and the King and Lancelot partook of this sacred repast. The King then put into operation a plot. His daughter was dispatched to a castle near by, and shortly after Lancelot was led to it by her duenna Brisane, thinking that he would see the Queen Guenevere. Instead, he was given a philtre which so muddled his wits that King Pelles' trick worked, and his daughter by the loss of her virginity conceived, much to her satisfaction, the perfect virgin knight, Galahad.

To some this *conte drolatique* will seem absurd, to others sacrilegious. But the author should not be judged too severely, for, given the traditions he had to work with, he could not have done much better. Lancelot must be faithful to Guenevere. He must father an illegitimate son on the Grail Bearer. This could occur only if he were deceived into the belief that he was lying with the Queen. These traditions had to be reconciled with a form of the Grail legend which was very different from that employed by Chrétien and his continuators, and which involved King Pelles in the deception of Lancelot and the deflowering of his own daughter. The attempt to amalgamate these *données* could not but result in absurdity; it even produced what seems like a travesty on the birth of Christ, since Galahad, the offspring of the union, was destined to play a messianic role in the *Quest*. Of course, the author was far from intending a mockery of anything so sacrosanct, but the resemblance is still there.

It was probably this same conscientious but not over-intelligent author who wrote the scenes which are consequent on the begetting of Galahad and which eventually lead up to his departure for the court of Arthur at Camelot at the age of fifteen. During the interval Sir Bors, Lancelot's cousin, visited Corbenic by chance, saw the baby Galahad, and learned the secret of his birth. Later the daughter of King Pelles turned up at court, much to Lancelot's embarrassment. A second time Brisane employed her craft to bring about their union. When Guenevere discovered her lover's infidelity and banished him, he was crazed with humiliation and grief. After long wanderings he came again by chance to Corbenic, was finally recognized by King Pelles' daughter and restored to sanity by the magic of the Grail. For a time he dwelt with her and his son on the Isle of Joy, but when Guenevere relented he returned to the court. In due time Pelles placed his grandchild in a nunnery to be educated, and there, we are told very briefly, Galahad remained till he was of an age to receive the order of knighthood. A hermit, who knew of the boy and his history, announced to King Arthur that at the next high feast of Pentecost the long-awaited hero who would bring to an end the adventures of the Grail would seek knighthood. It is not likely, in my opinion, that the author of this transitional material was the author of the *Quest*; it is too crude a mixture of the secular and the supernatural. But the two authors must have worked in some kind of collaboration, for they are mutually dependent; the work of the one presupposes the work of the other.

Needless to say, the sources of the *Prose Lancelot* are far too numerous to list. Chrétien's poems offered a convenient quarry, and his *Lancelot* was re-told and incorporated entire. The first two continuations of the *Perceval* were not neglected, neither was the Arthurian poem *Meraugis de Portlesguez*. Indeed, there was probably no romance of the cycle extant at the time in the French language which did not contribute. Some of these have long since been lost; more, I believe, than most scholars would allow. But all admit that the tale of Lancelot's kidnapping and fosterage by a fay must represent a lost form of the tradition preserved in the Swiss *Lanzelet*; and the extraordinary divergences of the Grail story from any version outside the Vulgate cycle can hardly be explained except by postulating the existence of a widely variant form of the legend which served as a basis.

The *Quest of the Holy Grail* begins without interruption or gap of any kind where the *Lancelot* leaves off. But one does not need to read more than a few pages before realizing that a new hand, a more sensitive and clear-sighted intelligence, has assumed control of the narrative.

A damsel of great beauty rode on horseback into Arthur's hall on the eve of Pentecost, and summoned Lancelot to the nunnery where Galahad had been reared, and there the father knighted the son, strange to say, without recognizing him. The next day, which was the 454th anniversary of the first Pentecost, Lancelot having returned, all the seats at the Round Table were filled except the Siege Perilous. At this solemn feast four kings and many barons served the first course. Suddenly the doors and window-shutters closed of themselves. None the less, an aged man in white mysteriously appeared, accompanied by a young knight in red arms. He greeted the company with the words 'Peace be with you', and announced to the King that he was bringing with him the Knight Desired, descended from King David and related to Joseph of Arimathea. Thereupon he led the young knight to the Siege Perilous, in which no one had dared to sit for fear of disaster. The knight seated himself without suffering any harm, and dismissed his escort, bidding him convey his salutations to King Pelles and the Fisher King. Thus Galahad passed the test of the Siege Perilous, was welcomed by all, and was hailed by Gawain as one sent by God to deliver the land from great wonders and strange adventures. He then met successfully a second test, pulling out with ease from a block of stone a sword which Gawain and Perceval had failed to budge.

In this majestic scene there is no discordant note in spite of the fact that an ancient pagan story provided the theme. In Chapter 1 it was pointed out that traditions of the Irish god Lugh were known to the Welsh and left marked traces on the French legend of Lancelot. In the story of Galahad's arrival at Arthur's court we find attached to Lancelot's son a narrative corresponding to that told of young Lugh in the ninth-century saga, the *Second Battle of Moytura*. First note that, according to a gloss on the Irish text, Lugh had the peculiar solar property of taking on a red colour from sunset to morning. On his arrival at the court of the god Nuada, he occupied the seat of the sage reserved for the wisest. He then demonstrated his superior strength by heaving a huge stone which was beyond the power of ordinary man to move. Accordingly he was recognized by the assembled court as the awaited hero who would free them from bondage. There are other correspondences between the coming of Galahad and the coming of Lugh to a royal court which should leave little doubt that the one is derived from the other.

The author, let us observe, has subtly imparted a Christian flavour to the pagan myth by introducing details from the gospel of St John. Twice, when the disciples were gathered together after the Resurrection, Jesus entered, though the doors were closed, and stood among them; and greeted them with the words 'Peace be with you!' By borrowing these two details from one of the most awe-inspiring appearances of Christ after His death, the author created precisely the right atmosphere for the arrival of the Christ-knight Galahad.

An extraordinary instance of endowing a secular tradition with a Christian significance is the choice of the name Galahad, or, according to the French texts, Galaad. If, as was pointed out on an earlier page, Lancelot's son may originally have been called Galaain, or something similar, the author of the *Quest*, steeped as he was in the Holy Scriptures and commentaries thereon, could hardly avoid substituting the biblical name

Galaad. And if he had no such precedent, he must be credited with a touch of genius. For it has been shown by Pauphilet that the personal name Galaad in the Latin Bible of the Catholic Church was taken to mean 'heap of testimony', and that a Cistercian commentator on the Song of Solomon, iv, interpreted this as referring to the accumulated testimony of the prophets to Christ as the Messiah. The name Galaad, therefore, seemed miraculously fitted to the long-awaited knight, the predestined deliverer. It carried with it an aura of sanctity appropriate to the hero of the Grail quest.

It was Pauphilet, also, who demonstrated that the author was a monk of the great order of Cîteaux, founded in 1098 as a protest against the distractions which beset the old and wealthy Benedictine monasteries—the preoccupation with elaborate ceremonial, the spending of money and time on costly decoration, the business of running a large household and maintaining widely scattered properties. Though theoretically cut off from the sordid concerns and pleasures of the world, the Benedictine monk found both the outer world and the affairs of his own community cutting too deeply into the time allotted to prayer and contemplation. The hungry soul starved; the mystic rebelled; the result was the Cistercian order.

Its great apostle was St Bernard of Clairvaux, who, by a sort of paradox, combined the life of mystic rapture with a life of vigorous reaction. On the one hand, he composed some of the classics of the inner life, including sermons on the Song of Solomon, and on the other was the adviser of kings and popes, and the prime mover of the Second Crusade. In the course of the twelfth and thirteenth centuries, partly as a result of his influence, Cistercian houses multiplied prodigiously. The ruins of such typical abbeys as Tintern and Fountains express by their remoteness from towns and the absence of decorative sculpture the austere ideal of their founders. Today the Trappists, an offshoot of the Cistercians, carry that ideal even further.

The evidence for Cistercian authorship is spread through the *Quest*. We meet with no black monks, Benedictines, but only with a white hermit, white monks, and white abbeys—the

Cistercian habit was white. The stages through which Lancelot passes before he obtains absolution from his sin with Guenevere are those which are systematically set forth in a manual of confession by Nicholas of Clairvaux, possibly a friend of our author, and surely bound by the same vows. Picture, then, the author as a monk in a white robe, bending over a desk in a scriptorium or cloister, transforming the rough materials of chivalric fiction into an allegory of the search for God's grace.

'Grace' is a key-word; it means in medieval theology and hence, of course, in the *Quest*, the unmerited favour or love of God. An evidence of this favour is the sacrament of the mass of which all Christians, truly repentant and absolved, may partake. Thus the Grail, here identified with the sacramental dish from which Christ ate the paschal lamb at the Last Supper, is taken as a symbol of God's grace. Another manifestation of grace, according to the Book of Acts, was the descent of the Holy Spirit upon the apostles at the first Christian Pentecost. Thus it is that when the author comes to describe the appearance of the Grail to the knights of the Round Table, late on the day of Pentecost—the same day as that on which Galahad met the tests of the Siege Perilous and the sword in the stone—he makes it clear not only that this was an anniversary recalling the earlier solemn occasion, but also that it signified the gift of divine grace, symbolized by the Grail.

Many readers of Malory will remember his faithful and inspired rendering of this scene, which I here briefly recall as it is told in the French source. Like the apostles, the knights of Arthur's household were assembled in the great hall. Instead of the sound of a rushing wind and the tongues of fire, there was a clap of thunder and a brilliant shaft of light. Then all were 'illumined by the grace of the Holy Spirit'. Forthwith, veiled in white samite, the Grail floated in through the door, and, passing along the tables, supplied at each place whatever viands each knight desired. The Grail vanished, and the King said: 'Lords, we ought to have great joy, since our Lord has shown us such a great sign of His love as to feed us on this high day with His grace.'

Few will deny that as a symbol of God's grace the volant vessel is more appropriate than a chalice or cup borne by so frail a woman as the daughter of King Pelles. Was this change the result of pure ratiocination? Was there no warrant for it in tradition? Just as the Grail maiden can be traced back to Irish myth, so too can the concept of self-moving vessels of plenty; and this concept turns up in two other accounts of the Grail. Once more, then, the author of the *Quest* has sublimated the material supplied by Celtic tradition. To quote a deeply perceptive dictum from Pauphilet's commentary:

> The great originality of our romancer lies in having felt, at the same time, the truly captivating charm of the Celtic tales, and the incomplete satisfaction which they afford to the spirit. . . . Everything is infused with the tantalizing poetry of chance, irrationality, and dream. But what is the meaning of these stories? Why does this happen, and not that? The imagination is ravished, but the intelligence is affronted; it endeavours to bring order into this charming chaos. The author of the *Quest* was far from suspecting that the stuff had not always been a meaningless phantasmagoria, and that these curious tales were for the most part the distorted expression of ancient pagan beliefs. But he had the rare perspicacity to understand that in the state in which his French contemporaries became acquainted with the wonder world of the Celts, it was empty. What he introduced into it was, naturally, his Christian conception of the universe and of Man.

The scenes which follow the Pentecostal visit of the Grail to Camelot are of a different cast; the supernatural is replaced by the natural; the Celtic pattern fades out. But one still recognizes the master hand in the description of the anguish of Arthur at the break-up of his order; the grief of the ladies at the message of the hermit Nascien, forbidding them to accompany their lords on the hazardous enterprise; the dialogue between Guenevere and Galahad on the embarrassing subject of his parentage; her parting words with Lancelot, beginning with passionate reproaches and ending with sorrowful blessings; the cavalcade winding through the streets of Camelot, watched by tearful crowds. Whoever wrote these passages was no harsh ascetic to whom normal human feelings were alien, but a man sensitive and tender.

Take his sympathetic treatment of Lancelot. When the notorious lover is called on by a hermit to confess, he proudly boasts of his paramour: 'It is she who has given me plenteously gold and silver, and rich gifts, which I have then bestowed on poor knights. It is she who has raised me to the great luxury and high estate in which I am. It is she for whose love I have done the great deeds of prowess of which all the world speaks. It is she who has led me from poverty to wealth, and from misery to all earthly good fortune.' The man who wrote those ringing sentences, was he at heart as stern a moralist as St Jerome? There can be no doubt that he condemned, in all sincerity, the sin, but that he felt with the sinner. When Lancelot has renounced the Queen, has been absolved and done penance, he is at last vouchsafed a vision of the Grail and of the Holy Trinity at the elevation of the Host. Since this is a privilege accorded to no other repentant sinner, it is clear that the author of the *Quest* did not altogether repudiate the values of the world. There is here something of the same ambivalence which one finds in Chaucer's *Troilus and Criseyde*, where the hero-lover is praised as an example of moral virtue, Venus is the 'verray cause of hele and of gladnesse', and yet at the end Troilus himself looks down in scorn on this wretched world and the blind lust that may not last.

What of Galahad as a character? Many critics have seen in him a figure so consistently triumphant, so closely assimilated to divine perfection, as to be more of an allegorical type than a creature of flesh and blood; and it is true that he has but one consuming desire, the mystic vision. However, he is no scornful Pharisee, but humble and affectionate, rejoicing in the companionship of Perceval and Bors, living with his father Lancelot in loving harmony. When they are obliged to part, the son addresses his father: 'Fair sweet sir, I do not know whether I shall ever see you again. I commend you to the true body of Jesus Christ, and may He keep you in His service.' And the very last words Galahad utters before his soul leaves his body are: 'Bors, greet my lord Lancelot, my father, as soon as you see him.'

Much of the book is taken up by the experiences of the lesser figures. Gawain and Hector, since they neglect confession, have no adventures. When Perceval and Bors are tempted, though near to yielding, they emerge victorious. There are many visions, and each is expounded by a knowledgeable hermit. Some of these exegetics seem too banal and artificial to please the taste of any but those who share the author's ardour; but even those who do not may well concede the clarity and charm of the style.

There is one long episode so bizarre and so typical of medieval symbology that it cannot be overlooked. Galahad, Bors, Perceval, and Perceval's sister discover a mysterious ship, with not a soul aboard. A Chaldean inscription informs them that the vessel is Faith. Entering, they see a magnificent bed, into the frame of which three spindles of red, white, and green wood have been introduced in the form of a cross. At the foot of the bed is a sword of fine workmanship, attached to a belt of coarse hemp. Perceval's sister, who takes the place of the usual hermit as expositor, tells the story and the meaning of the sword, the ship, and the spindles. The vessel was built by Solomon, and since Solomon was the builder of the Temple, the vessel symbolizes the Church of the Old Testament. The three spindles were made from three states of the Tree of Knowledge, and, since the cross of Calvary was made of the same wood, they transform the vessel into the Church of the New Testament. The sword, according to Ephesians, vi, 17, is the Word of God, that is, the Scriptures. The hempen belt indicates the inferior inspiration of the Old Testament. When Perceval's virgin sister replaces it with a girdle in which silk, gold thread, and strands of her own hair are intertwined the Old Testament is replaced by the New. To some readers this curious description of Solomon's ship may seem an example of perverted ingenuity. But for others it will hold something of the fascination of Herbert's poetry, or Donne's, so fresh is the imagery, so hallowed are the associations.

The most majestic scene in the romance is set in the Grail castle and is well known to many through the beautiful and faithful rendering by Malory. Of the old pagan traditions about the entertainment of the hero in the mansion of a god five traces remain: the setting is not a chapel but a castle hall; there is the bleeding spear, recalling the spear of Lugh; there is the dish which provides the food one most desires; the castle is named Corbenic, which can most plausibly be explained as a corruption of *corbenoit*, 'blessed horn', that is, the magic drinking horn of Bran; there is the Maimed King, whose prototype was the wounded Bran.

Entirely oblivious of the origin of this material, the author, having adopted the belief that the dish, the Grail, was a sacramental vessel, proceeded to develop the already Christianized tradition of the banquets of Bran into a eucharistic feast. He embodied in it three familiar concepts: 1, The Divine Liturgy, that is the participation of the Heavenly Host and the Church Triumphant in the celebration of the mass. Thus it is that angels bring in the holy objects, and that the son of Joseph of Arimathea, Josephes, who had died three hundred years before, descends from the skies, and officiates. 2, The Apostolic Communion, a re-enactment of the Last Supper. This accounts for the unexpected participation of nine newly arrived knights in the rite, together with Galahad, Perceval, and Bors, and for the administering of the Host by Christ Himself. 3, The miracle of Transubstantiation made visible. Thus we are told that at the elevation of the mass-wafer a fiery-faced child entered it, and later Christ, showing the wounds of the crucifixion, emerged from the Grail.

It is then that the Saviour addressed the twelve knights in these memorable words:

'My knights and my servants and my loyal sons, who

in this mortal life have become spiritual, and have sought me so long that I cannot hide myself longer from you; it is fitting that ye shall see a part of my secrets and my mysteries. For ye have accomplished so much that ye are seated at my table where never a knight has eaten since the time of Joseph of Arimathea. . . . Now hold and receive the high food which ye have so long desired, and for which ye have toiled so much.' When He had served all the twelve, He asked Galahad: 'Son, pure and purged as far as any earthly man can be, knowest thou what I hold between my hands?' 'No,' said he, 'if ye do not tell me.' 'This is,' said He, 'the dish from which Jesus Christ ate the lamb the day of the Passover with His disciples. It is the dish which has served to their joy all those whom I have found in my service. It is the dish which no unbeliever has ever looked upon without being sorely harmed. And because it has served every one agreeably, it is rightly called the Holy Grail. . . .'

After this rapturous repast, the three elect, accompanied by the holy vessel, are wafted in Solomon's ship to the land of Sarras (apparently Palestine, then occupied by Saracens). They are at first persecuted and imprisoned, but in time they are released and Galahad is crowned king. On the anniversary of his coronation he expires after a supreme vision of the Grail. Perceval dies in his turn, and Bors alone returns to Camelot.

In spite of occasional flaws and arid patches, the *Quest* is one of the noblest romances of the Middle Ages.

As in turning from the *Lancelot* to the *Quest* one feels a sharp change in atmosphere and artistry, so, too, the passage from the latter to the *Mort Artu* is marked by an equally curious shift. Although some critics still claim the authorship for Walter Map, he has become a much more worldly Walter. Religious allegory is replaced by realism. We hear no more of Corbenic, but, instead, of Winchester, Dover, Edinburgh

(Taneborc), the River Humber, the Tower of London, and Salisbury Plain. There are no white monks, and hermits play a minor part. Lancelot relapses, Bors seems untouched by his mystic experiences.

The new author, perhaps identical with the composer of some of the best parts of the *Lancelot*, undertook the formidable task of bridging the gap between the well-developed theme of the adulterous but idealized loves of Lancelot and Guenevere, on the one hand, and the altogether separate tradition of the treason of Modred and the fall of Arthur, on the other. What he took from such sources as Wace or *Tristan* he greatly modified, and the book is for the most part pure invention. He succeeded in achieving a remarkable unity, a series of events linked by a chain of causality. Although much of the *Mort* is familiar to us through Malory and the *Idylls of the King*, a brief summary seems necessary.

Lancelot resumes his old liaison with the Queen. Attending incognito a tournament at Winchester, he rashly wears on his helm the sleeve of the Maid of Astolat (Escalot), and then, when seriously wounded, is nursed by her. The rumour gets about that he has given her his heart, and the Queen is furiously jealous. Only when a barge floats down to Camelot, bearing the body of the Maid and a letter which proves the rumour false, and after Lancelot has saved the Queen from burning on the false charge of poisoning a knight, does she receive him back into her favour.

Meantime, Arthur has learned of the liaison from a gallery of autobiographic paintings which Lancelot had carefully executed and carelessly left behind on the walls of Morgan le Fay's castle. With the King's connivance Agravain and a group of knights trap the lovers together. Lancelot escapes, but Guenevere is again condemned to be burned. Arriving in the nick of time, Lancelot rescues her and takes her to his castle of Joyous Garde; but by a fateful mischance he cuts down, without recognizing him, Gawain's favourite brother, Gaheriet. As a result, Gawain, who had been hitherto Lancelot's staunch friend, became his implacable enemy.

This unjustified but natural hatred is one of the major links in the chain of causation which ends in catastrophe.

It was Gawain who, even after Lancelot had returned the Queen to Arthur and Arthur had received her back, would not abandon his quarrel, and it was Gawain who incited his uncle to revive the war and attack Lancelot in his territory across the Channel. He provoked Lancelot to a duel and was severely wounded in the head. Arthur then withdrew his force to Meaux. Threatened with an invasion of Gaul by the Romans, he defeated them and killed the Emperor.

But, meanwhile, his son by incest, Modred, has seized the opportunity offered by the absence of the King and Gawain on the Continent to mount the throne. On the very day of victory over the Romans a messenger from Guenevere, who has taken refuge in the Tower of London, brings the news of Modred's treachery to Arthur. He hastens back with his army and crosses to Dover. There Gawain succumbs to the wound which Lancelot has given him, but, realizing at last the catastrophic consequences of his behaviour, he sends a dying message to Lancelot imploring forgiveness.

Though deprived of the aid of his greatest knights, and though warned by visions and other portents, Arthur stubbornly led his forces to Salisbury Plain. There (not in Cornwall) he joined battle with Modred and his Saxon allies. As the day of carnage drew to a close he drove his spear through his son's body, but was desperately wounded by his son. There followed the memorable scene of the casting away of Excalibur into the lake, and this was followed by the departure of Arthur by sea in a barge filled with ladies, including Morgan le Fay, his sister. Three days later, a survivor of the battle, entering a chapel, saw the newly made tomb of Arthur.

Guenevere took the veil. Lancelot returned with a host and avenged his lord's death on the two sons of Modred. Then, as Dante put it, he 'lowered the sails of his mundane labours' and became a hermit. When he died four years later his body was interred in the same tomb as Galehot's and angels bore his soul to heaven.

Thus the tragic pattern is worked out with care and 'high seriousness'. The author, it is interesting to observe, implicates three forces as the agents of doom. There is an ineluctable Fate, represented by a vision of the goddess Fortuna and her wheel and by an inscription on a rock forecasting the outcome of the battle of Salisbury Plain. Less clearly defined as a controlling force is the retributive justice of God, though it may be inferred in the fate of Arthur, guilty, though unwitting, of the sin of incest. Third, and most important, is the determinant role of character. It is the unjustified and rancorous hatred of Gawain for Lancelot which contributes largely to the downfall of Arthur and his order. It is Arthur's stubborn pride which causes him to ignore omens and warnings, and, like Julius Caesar, to invite his death.

Indeed, characterization is perhaps the forte of the author of the *Mort Artu*. There are such simple but very real figures as the Maid of Astolat, infatuated by the elderly but still magnificent Lancelot, and as Modred, lustful, deceitful, but courageous. More variable and complex is Guenevere, shifting from the extreme of jealous anger to the extreme of passionate abandon, meekly leaving the joys of Joyous Garde rather than injure her lover and prolong the war, exhibiting in her defiance of Modred resourcefulness and courage. Then there is Lancelot, who when his secret affair comes into the open is defiant and denies the accusations, but who sends his lady back to the King when he realizes the consequences of keeping her, and who not only spares Arthur and Gawain in combat but even offers to give up all his possessions to Gawain and go into exile, rather than prolong the war. This is a very different Lancelot, of course, from the Lancelot of either of the two preceding books—the unscrupulous deceiver of his lord and friend and the penitent sinner. But there is no necessary inconsistency, rather a growth in magnanimity and in awareness of consequences.

And there is a magnanimity in the author himself. It is an unusual Frenchman who would compose the farewell which Lancelot murmured as he left the shores of Logres behind:

'O sweet land, full of all blessings, in which my spirit and my life forever dwell, blessed be thou by the mouth of Him who is called Jesus Christ, and blessed be all those who remain in thee, be they my friends or my foes! May they have peace! may they have rest! . . . Certes they will have them, for no one could be in so sweet a country as this is and not be happier than anywhere else. I say it who have proved it, for as long as I lived there good fortune befell me more abundantly than it would in any other land.'

One appreciates the *Mort Artu* the more when one realizes that the complex and admirable plot is, except for the borrowing from Wace (the war with the Romans, the treason of Modred, the last battle), largely original. Of the old Celtic tradition little remains. The increase in Gawain's strength towards midday, often mentioned in the French romances, and its subsequent decline suggest that his prototype was a solar hero like Cuchulainn. Arthur's dying address to Excalibur and his prayer that it may never come into unworthy hands bear a marked resemblance to the speech of the Irish hero, Fergus mac Leite, to his people regarding the fate of his sword Caladcolg, a resemblance most noteworthy since both heroes were lying, grievously wounded, beside a lake. Arthur's departure in the barge with Morgan le Fay reflects the Breton legend which Layamon had recorded twenty-five years or more earlier. But of Arthur's healing there is no word; instead we read of his burial in the Noire or Veire Chapele. That this change was the result of the faked 'discovery' of the bones of Arthur in 1191 at Glastonbury can hardly be doubted. Is it possible that the words *Noire* or *Veire Chapele* were not pure inventions, but represent a curious corruption of *Ile de Voire*, 'Isle of Glass', which was taken to refer to Glastonbury?

Though a comparison of the *Mort Artu* with Malory's last books would probably convince most critics of the superior art of the later romance, yet the earlier is a masterpiece in its own right—a masterpiece of tone, characterization, and design.

JOSEPH OF ARIMATHEA
AND GLASTONBURY

OF ALL the strange phenomena which perplex the student of Arthurian literature, perhaps the strangest is the association of the Grail, which appeared in Britain in Arthur's time, with Joseph of Arimathea, who, according to the Scriptures, took down the body of Christ from the cross and laid it in the sepulchre at least four hundred and fifty years before. Chrétien evidently knew nothing of this association when he wrote his *Perceval* about 1180; but within the next half-century a considerable literature, including the long French prose romance, the *History of the Holy Grail*, which forms the first book in the Vulgate cycle, came into existence, relating how Joseph had acquired the vessel, what miracles had it performed, how it had been transported to Britain and had been preserved there until Arthur's time in the haunted castle of Corbenic. Strange, too, that in the fifteenth century Joseph's evangelizing mission was accepted as historic fact. Even today there seem to be more than a few who take it seriously.

Let us attempt to solve this riddle and see how the legend grew up, and then, if possible, see why, even at the risk of seeming too venturesome.

The legend of Joseph of Arimathea begins with the historic fact, mentioned by all four gospels, that he asked Pilate for the body of Christ, took it down from the cross, and laid it in the sepulchre. St John's gospel adds that Nicodemus, another disciple, assisted in the task. By the end of the fourth century, it seems, an apocryphal work known as the *Gospel of Nicodemus* gave a much expanded account of the trial of Christ and the events following the crucifixion. St Luke's words about the descent from the cross and the entombment are quoted. Then we are told how the Jews, angry with Joseph of Arimathea because of this action, promptly placed him in a house without windows, sealed the door, and set guards. But when they opened the door on Easter Sunday their prisoner had vanished. Alarmed by this and by news of the Resurrection, the Jews, repentant, sought for Joseph and found him in his home at Arimathea. They invited him to Jerusalem, and there, before the council, he told how the house in which he was confined was lifted into the air, how he fell down, and how Jesus then appeared, kissed him, and led him by the hand back to Arimathea.

Other apocryphal narratives prolong the imprisonment until the fall of Jerusalem (A.D. 70). According to one version of the *Avenging of the Saviour*, when the city was captured and a thick wall was broken through, an old man was discovered, who revealed himself as Joseph of Arimathea, miraculously sustained with light and food from heaven. Another version, after relating the discovery of Joseph and Nicodemus, goes on to say that a messenger of the Emperor Tiberius learned that a woman named Veronica possessed the imprint of Jesus's face on a cloth, and so he brought her with him to Rome. There, as soon as Tiberius saw and adored the image, he was healed of fever, ulcers, and nine kinds of leprosy!

Thus Joseph of Arimathea was already a prominent subject for pious legend when Arthur was campaigning against the Saxons. And it was this material which in the twelfth century was available for amalgamation with the Christianized Celtic stories of the platter and horn of Bran.

What probably represents a very early stage in this amalgamation is a passage of about a hundred and seventy-five lines interpolated in the First Continuation of Chrétien's *Perceval*. The Grail has just been described as floating about, without any butler to hold it, and providing Gawain and the others with an abundance of food and wine. Then we are told that Joseph had caused this vessel to be made, and that, when he learned of Christ's death, he went and collected in it the blood which dripped from His feet. Going to Pilate, he begged the holy body; he then took it down from the cross, and deposited it in the tomb. The Jews imprisoned him in a tower, but in answer to his prayer the tower rose up and left him free once more. Thereupon the Jews banished him and his friends, including Nicodemus. Before departing, Joseph secretly took a sculpture of the Lord's head which Nicodemus had made, cast it into the sea at Jaffa, and commended it to God's care. (In fact, known as the *Volto Santo*, the wooden bust is still venerated at Lucca.) Joseph and his company set sail and after some wandering reached the White Isle, a part of England. When the natives attacked them and starvation threatened, the Grail supplied them with wine and food. After Joseph's death it remained in the charge of his descendants, including the Rich Fisher.

Though it has been asserted that this interpolation is a late and unimportant version of the combined story of Joseph and the Grail, it presents too many differences from all the well-known versions to be accepted as a derivative from any of them. Most significant is the fact that while the rest postpone the liberation of Joseph till after the fall of Jerusalem, thus showing the influence of the *Avenging of the Saviour*, the interpolation, following the *Gospel of Nicodemus*, tells of his prompt miraculous delivery in answer to prayer, and shows no influence of other apocrypha. It seems reasonable to conclude that it represents the earliest stage of the legend of Joseph and the Grail which we possess, and, though not the source of the other texts, resembles the simple version from which they were elaborated. Who the author of this hypothetical source was, it would be fascinating to discover, but beyond the presumption that he was a French cleric, roughly contemporary with Chrétien de Troyes, all is a blank.

The earliest of the well-known forms of the legend is a poem usually called *Joseph of Arimathea* or the *Metrical Joseph*, composed by a Burgundian from near the Swiss border, Robert de Boron, probably not long before or after his friend,

Gautier de Monbéliard, departed for Italy in 1199. Though the pious content of the poem would imply clerical author-ship, Robert may have been a knight, for his style is crude and his narrative is marred by gross blunders which can be explained only as due to misreadings of an earlier text. In fact, he invokes the authority of a 'grant livre' written by great scholars concerning the secret of the Grail. His was therefore not an original work, but the muddled redaction of an earlier and clearer narrative, now, unluckily, lost. If sceptics find it difficult to believe in such lost sources they might consider that not a single twelfth-century manuscript of Chrétien de Troyes or Marie de France has come down to us, and yet they must have existed.

One of the most astonishing facts about Robert's poem is that, though he identifies the Grail with the vessel in which the Lord made His sacrament at the Last Supper, and though it is the centre of interest, he omits from his account of the repast any mention of the sacrament. It is only after the Lord and the apostles have left that a Jew picks up the vessel and gives it to Pilate. Pilate, after the crucifixion, grants the request of Joseph of Arimathea, a mercenary soldier, for the body of the Crucified and also gives him the vessel. (Note that at only two places does Robert use the word *graal* of this vessel.) Joseph takes down the holy body from the cross with the aid of Nicodemus, collects in his vessel the blood oozing from the wounds, and lays the body in the tomb. Next follow the Descent into Hell and the Resurrection. The Jews, enraged at finding the empty sepulchre, fling Joseph into prison. To him the risen Christ appears in a great light, holding the precious vessel, gives it to him, and expounds the symbolism of the sacrament. The bread and wine are the Redeemer's flesh and blood; the tomb is the altar; the vessel is the chalice; the paten, which covers the chalice, is the tombstone.

Up to this point Robert's narrative is clearly compounded of the following elements: the Scriptures, the apocryphal Descent into Hell, the *Gospel of Nicodemus*, the matter associating Joseph with the eucharistic vessel, and the symbolical interpretation of the utensils, borrowed from Honorius of Autun.

The scene now shifts, and we detect the intrusion of material from the *Avenging of the Saviour*. Vespasian, son of the Roman emperor, is cured of leprosy by the portrait of Christ brought to Rome by Verrine (Veronica). He sets out for Judea to wreak vengeance on the Jews for the crucifixion, and there, in the course of his mission, he is led to the dungeon in which Joseph was confined and finds him hale and hearty, though without sustenance, and ready to expound the doctrine of the Fall and the Redemption. Vespasian proves an easy convert.

This part of the *Joseph* represents a variation on the *Avenging of the Saviour*, and it is this part, therefore, which rules out the possibility that the *Joseph* was the source of the interpolation summarized above.

The remainder of the poem no longer parallels the apocrypha; two characters never mentioned in them or the gospels are introduced: Joseph's sister Enygeus and her husband, alternatively named Hebron or Bron. They join the company of Christians which Joseph leads into exile, and their travels adumbrate vaguely the wanderings of the Jews in the wilderness. When some of the band are guilty of lust all are threatened with starvation. The divine voice instructs Joseph to make a replica of the table employed at the Last Supper. Bron is then to catch a fish; it is to be placed on the table opposite the holy vessel. When Joseph bids the people who have faith in the Trinity and have kept the commandments to sit and eat, only a part of them do so and are filled with the desire of their hearts. The rest are excluded and feel nothing. Because of the pleasure the vessel bestows, it is called *graal* (a false derivation from *agreer*, 'to please'). One of the sinners tries to occupy an empty place at the table and is swallowed by the earth—a biblical reminiscence.

In the course of time Bron's wife bears twelve sons. Eleven of them marry, but the twelfth, Alain, declares that he would rather be flayed. Because of this resolve, Joseph selects this nephew to be leader of his brothers, to guide them and their families to the farthest west, there to preach Christ. A certain Petrus also chooses to go west to the vales of Avaron, and there await the coming of the son of Alain—Alain, the celibate! Joseph entrusts the vessel itself to Bron, henceforth to be called the Rich Fisher, and imparts to him the secrets which the Lord had revealed to him in prison. Bron also is to go west, await the coming of his grandson, and then convey the vessel to him. In succession Alain, Petrus, Bron, and their companies depart, but Joseph remains in the land where he was born.

Robert de Boron concluded without relating the missionary efforts of Alain, Petrus, and Bron, but with a promise to do so if he could find a book to supply the necessary information— another confession that his was not an original work. Moreover, he referred tantalizingly to the many tales told about the good Fisher—evidence of an oral tradition about Bron.

In the last section of Robert's *Joseph* one recognizes certain elements already discussed in connection with Chrétien's *Perceval* and the *Quest of the Holy Grail*. The title Rich Fisher corresponds to the title Fisher King in Chrétien; the empty place at the Grail table which will not tolerate an unchaste occupant matches the Siege Perilous in the *Quest*, which awaits the coming of the virgin Galahad. It was shown that Chrétien's maimed Fisher King had his prototype in the wounded King Bran of the *mabinogi*, and it is therefore no mere coincidence that Robert's Rich Fisher is named Bron. Nor can it be an accident that whereas Bran directed his followers to dwell for a time at Harlech on the west coast of Wales and then proceed to the Isle of Grassholm, the westernmost point in Wales, the Rich Fisher, Bron, should journey to the Occident.

It therefore seems clear, first, that the last part of the *Joseph* contains genuine Celtic material; secondly, that its true nature has been deliberately and successfully disguised by a face-lifting process which makes it look like an apocryphum; and, thirdly, that the material has been shifted from Arthur's time, where it belonged, to the first century. Why this shift? Obviously, because the Grail had been equated with a vessel of the Last Supper, and its keeper with Joseph of Arimathea.

The crucial question remains: Why was Joseph chosen as the first custodian of the vessel, when there was nothing in the gospels or the apocrypha to suggest it? It is easy to reply that no reason or cause is needed to account for the choice other than some cleric's caprice. But is it likely that a mere whim was reponsible for making the audacious association of a talismanic vessel of Arthur's time with one of the early disciples of Christ? Is there not a more adequate explanation?

It is a most remarkable fact that the very same hypothesis previously advanced for the connection of the Grail with the mass-wafer in Chrétien's poem would also account for the association of the Grail with Joseph. The unsuitable and un-canonical introduction of the sacred Host on a platter borne by a damsel was plausibly explained as due to misinterpretation of the French word *cors* as 'body', and specifically as the Corpus Christi. The choice of Joseph as the first custodian of the Grail can be explained just as reasonably as due to the misinterpretation of *cors* as 'body', this time, however, equated with the body which Joseph took down from the cross and placed in his tomb.

Once the mistake about Bran's drinking horn, translated into French as *cors*, had led to the identification of Bran's counterpart with Joseph, it was the next step to equate the magic platter of Bran with a suitably holy dish. And there was the dish of the Last Supper, mentioned in Matthew, xxv, 23, lying ready to hand. From that point on it was only necessary to continue Joseph's career with matter from the *Gospel of Nicodemus*, to bring him to England, and to account for the preservation of his relic down to Arthur's time. And that is what we found in the interpolation.

The source of Robert's poem represents a later stage when its author was faced by the contradictory tradition that the custodian of the Grail was named, not Joseph, but Bron. He seems to have reconciled the two claims by the simple expedient of making Bron Joseph's brother-in-law and successor. At least, that is what Robert tells us.

Mystery surrounds Petrus and his journey to the vales of

Avaron. All that one can say is that in 1191, if not before, Avalon was equated with Glastonbury, and that there was a tradition as early as 1000 that the first preachers of Christ in Britain found at Glastonbury a church consecrated to the Virgin. It is not unlikely that a faint echo of this tradition is to be detected in the voyage of Petrus to the west, to the vales of Avaron.

Some readers may consider this detailed analysis of a poem as confused and crude as Robert de Boron's *Joseph* a gross misapportionment of space. Why not dismiss it in a few words as the work of a stupid rimester and leave it at that? If purely aesthetic values were all that mattered, Robert would deserve no more attention. But his *Joseph* has to be understood if one is to interpret correctly the works of the greater artists who dealt with the legend of Joseph of Arimathea. To shirk the task of interpreting the poem in its historical and literary setting is to abandon the field to every amateur with a theory.

The longest and most widely read of all the romances concerned with the origins of the mysterious vessel is the *History of the Holy Grail*, which forms the first book in the Vulgate cycle. It opens with the claim that it is a transcript of a book which Christ Himself had written and delivered to a hermit 717 years after the Passion. If the claim were true, it would reflect severely not only on the Lord's veracity but also on His talents as a writer of fiction. As we read on, we learn that the hermit was afflicted with doubts about the Trinity, but, after being rapt up to heaven and having a vision of the Three-in-One, he was restored to orthodoxy. It is hard to decide whether this was the author's private joke, or whether he was touched in the head.

Actually he must have been an ecclesiastic who composed his tome about 1230 in order to illuminate the antecedents of the vessel which figured so largely in the *Quest*. Scholars generally agree that he followed Robert's *Joseph*, though with considerable changes, as far as the poem went; but there is reason to suppose that he also used Robert's source, for he avoids Robert's blundering interpretations of his source. He does not confuse the Grail with a chalice and never employs the form Hebron. Like the author of the *Quest*, he equates the vessel with the dish (*escuele*) from which the Lord partook of the lamb at the Last Supper.

This brings up the puzzling subject of the relation of the *History of the Holy Grail* to the *Quest*, two parts of the Vulgate cycle which are so interdependent that investigators of an older generation attributed them to the same author. The *Quest* contains references to what, judging by the evidence of the text, must have been an earlier work, dealing with Evalach, Mordrain, Nascien, and Josephes, son of Joseph of Arimathea. These references correspond closely to what the *History of the Holy Grail* tells us of these characters, and yet, scholars are agreed, the *History* was composed later than the *Quest*. What is the answer to this puzzle? There must have been a common source, now lost—an elaboration and continuation of Robert de Boron's *Joseph*, which was itself expanded into the *Vulgate History*, but only after it had provided the basis for the references in the *Quest*. Thus the harmony between the two books of the Vulgate cycle can be accounted for, at least partially; and a further harmonization may have been carried out by the final redactor or redactors of the grandiose work.

One of the chief divergences of the *History of the Holy Grail* from Robert's *Joseph* is the treatment of Bron. He is not even mentioned until the transport of the Grail company to Britain, and thereafter plays an inferior role. Not he, but his son Alain, catches the fish and is called the Rich Fisher. On the other hand, Joseph is not left behind but plays a great part in the evangelization of Britain. His son Josephes takes over Bron's place as keeper of the Grail and as head of the mission. The creation of this new character was demanded by the fact that Joseph and Bron were not in holy orders. The glory of spreading the faith in the West must not fall to married laymen, but to a celibate and preferably a bishop. A long passage is devoted to the initiation of Josephes into the rites and secrets of the eucharist and the symbolism of the episcopal vestments. In what to some will seem a repulsive manner he is convinced of the Trinity; as he is celebrating mass, the bread turns into a child, and when he cuts the child into three pieces, in accordance with divine instructions, it becomes one again as he swallows it. Qualified by these supernal experiences, Josephes becomes an apostle to the Gentiles, rivalling St Paul.

First, the land of Sarras, conceived of as near Egypt, then Orcanie (the Orkney Isles), then England, Wales, Scotland, and the Terre Foraine are brought into the Christian fold. Sometimes an exposition of the faith is sufficient; sometimes a miracle is required; sometimes there is a holy war. Of course, visions abound: Christ appears in the form of a stag, followed by four lions representing the evangelists; a great lake flowing out in nine streams signifies Celidoine and his nine lineal descendants culminating in Lancelot and Galahad. There are numerous imprisonments and temptations. Four characters—Josephes, Joseph, King Galaphes of the Terre Foraine, and Pellean—are at various times wounded in the thighs with a spear. Robert's Petrus turns up as Pierre, but instead of going to the vales of Avaron to await the son of Alain, as Robert predicted, he is carried by chance to Orcanie, converts the heathen king, marries his daughter, and becomes the ancestor of Gawain. The last pages cover rapidly the reigns of the royal keepers of the Grail who succeeded Alain. Thus we are brought down to King Pelles, the grandfather of Galahad; and thus the author of the *History of the Holy Grail* filled out the chronological gap between apostolic times and the age of Arthur.

Very little of all this, except the Grail itself and the motif of a wound in the thighs, bears any relation to Celtic tradition. But one may suspect that an old heathenish belief lies behind the account of the Waste Land, which is found in both the *History of the Holy Grail* and the *Quest*. Once upon a time in the realm of Logres King Varlan inflicted a fatal blow on the most Christian king Lambor with the sword of the strange girdle, and as a consequence no wheat sprouted, no trees bore fruit, and no fish inhabited the waters. Hence it was called the Waste

Land. Obviously we are presented here in romanticized form with the superstition that a sympathetic relation exists between the life of a king and the vital forces of his kingdom.

As a work of art, or as an expression of religious feeling, the *History of the Holy Grail* cannot compare with the *Quest*. A crude sensationalism is its dominating tone; conventional thaumaturgy and crass dogmatism constitute its religion. Still, one cannot help admiring, with reservations, the ingenuity with which the author, supplemented by the final redactor of the Vulgate cycle, provided an answer to the questions which a reader of the *Quest* might ask—a prehistory of Josephes, Mordrain, Pelles; an explanation of such traditional phrases as the Maimed King, the Waste Land, and so forth. Successfully fitted into the Vulgate cycle, the *History of the Holy Grail* became the standard account of the origins of the vessel, and was translated into English, Dutch, Spanish, and Portuguese. It was the basis of the claim made by the English delegates at the great Church councils of Pisa, Constance, Siena, and Basel in the fifteenth century, to precedence over the delegates of France and Spain. It is the source of the modern popular belief that Joseph of Arimathea actually came to Glastonbury and founded the first Christian mission in the British Isles.

Some readers of this book may be surprised to learn that the *History of the Holy Grail*, though it gives an elaborate narrative of Joseph's mission, never mentions Glastonbury; that the *Joseph* of Robert de Boron, though it forecasts the arrival of Petrus at the vales of Avaron, presumably Glastonbury, restricts the activities of Joseph to the East. *Perlesvaus*, a French romance translated by Sebastian Evans into English, places the tombs of Joseph and Nicodemus in Britain and displays an acquaintance, though inaccurate, with the site of the abbey; but of any association between the Somerset house, on the one hand, and Joseph and the Grail, on the other, there is no trace.

In fact, the abbey cultivated, since the year 1000 at least, an entirely different story: the first preachers of Christ in Britain discovered at Glastonbury a church built by no man's hand and consecrated to the honour of the Virgin Mary. Until 1184 there stood on the precincts a church made of wattles, which may well have been a very early sanctuary. It was burned in the great fire of 1184, and the present chapel of St Mary takes its place. In the early thirteenth century, it was believed, according to the forged Charter of St Patrick, that twelve disciples of St Philip and St James built the old church at the bidding of the Archangel Michael. Not a word of Joseph of Arimathea, not a word of the Grail, not a word of Petrus and the vales of Avalon.

It must have come as a complete surprise and something of a shock when the *History of the Holy Grail* was called to the attention of the abbot of Glastonbury, and he read a history of the evangelization of Britain which bore little relation to the official account, and yet was full of corroborative detail, harmonized with the apocrypha, and even claimed at second hand a divine source. Apparently the evidence for the authenticity of the French romance was so strong that it could not be laughed away, and so a compromise was effected; Joseph was stated to be leader of the disciples whom St Philip sent from Gaul to Britain. Gradually, he was adopted as one of the chief patrons of the monastery. Search was made for his grave. In the fourteenth century a chapel was consecrated to him, a sculpture of the Deposition from the cross was placed in it, and an image of our Lady was in turn ascribed to his workmanship. From all over Somerset the sick flocked to his shrine and were miraculously cured. In 1502 or thereabouts a poem mentions three hawthorns which bear green leaves at Christmastide—the first mention of the Glastonbury thorn. But, though the French legend of Joseph came to be accepted as official not only by the monastery but also by the English hierarchy, yet one feature of the legend was never taken over. Strange to say, it was the Grail. So when one sees St Joseph depicted on rood-screen or in stained glass in the churches of the neighbourhood, he bears neither platter nor chalice, but two cruets filled with the blood and sweat of the Crucified.

MERLIN

In Chapter 3 there was brief mention of the two works, the *Prophecies of Merlin* and the *Life of Merlin*, which Geoffrey of Monmouth attached to that eerie and imposing figure of the Matter of Britain. And according to Geoffrey's *History of the Kings of Britain*, King Uther Pendragon would never have lain with Igerna in the castle of Tintagel, and Arthur would never have been born, had it not been for the magic arts of the wizard Merlin. Credited in the Dark Ages with the composition of obscure verses in Welsh, the mage had become renowned by the dawn of the Renaissance throughout western Christendom as a prophet of equal authority with Isaiah or the Sibyl. Let us, belatedly, trace the history of this extraordinary evolution.

In a sense, it begins with a blunder, for the latest authority declares that there never was a man called Myrddin (the Welsh form of Merlin) and that the name originated in a mistaken interpretation of the place-name Carmarthen as the *caer* (town) of Myrddin. This spurious etymology left its imprint on Geoffrey of Monmouth, who placed the boy Merlin at Carmarthen, and also on the local folklore of today, for an old tree-stump is the subject of a prophecy: 'When Merlin's tree shall tumble down, Then shall fall Carmarthen town.'

For reasons never to be known, the gift of prophecy was conferred on the purely imaginary Myrddin, and a Welsh poem of about 930 cites him as authority for vaticinations contained in it. Five or six poems attributed to Myrddin himself have come down to us from the succeeding period and pretend to forecast political events. But along with the forecasts are mingled references to the imaginary history of the imaginary bard. He was a madman who took part in the battle of Arderydd (which was actually fought near Carlisle in 573), and when his lord, King Gwenddolau, was killed, lost his reason. Hunted by the victor, Rhydderch, a historic King of Dumbarton, Myrddin has taken refuge in the wood of Celyddon in the Scottish Lowlands, enduring the rigours of winter with snow reaching to his hips and icicles in his hair, his only companion a pig. In another poem he utters prophecies in response to the questions of his sister Gwenddydd. Still another consists of a dialogue between Myrddin and the chief of bards, Taliesin.

How can one explain the fact that these Welsh poems show such specific knowledge of historic personages of four centuries or so earlier, and familiarity with a region so remote from South Wales? It now seems clear that the legend of Myrddin's madness and his life in the forest, which is implied in the poems, actually took shape in the Scottish Lowlands, not about Myrddin, who was quite unknown there, but about a legendary madman and prophet named Lailoken. This must have happened before the region was overwhelmed by the Angles. Britons fleeing south to Wales brought along with them their legendary and poetic heritage. Once this migration is realized, one can understand why traditions about such northern heroes as Drustan and Owain son of Urien turn up in Welsh literature. Why the legend of Lailoken was transferred to the illusory Merlin is a riddle unanswered, and will probably remain so.

There is no evidence in early Welsh poetry that Myrddin was associated in any way with Arthur, and this is natural, for Arthur was a southern hero. But apparently by the twelfth century the connection had been made, and news of Myrddin's soothsayings passed, together with tales of Arthur's prowess, into Anglo-Norman Britain and aroused enormous curiosity— a curiosity which, as we have seen, Geoffrey of Monmouth was quick to exploit. At first, he seems to have known little of the literature in the Welsh language about the seer, but lifted out of Nennius a tale about a prophetic boy named Ambrosius, rechristened him Merlin, and introduced the following episode into his *History*. Vortigern, King of Britain, fled before the Saxons to Snowdonia, and caused a strong tower to be erected on a site near Beddgelert, which can still be seen. But each night the foundations laid during the day sank into the earth. Advised by his wizards, the King sent messengers to find a boy without a father. At Carmarthen a boy was discovered whose mother, a princess of Dyved, divulged that no human being, but an incubus, had lain with her in her sleep and fathered the boy Merlin. The boy prodigy challenged the wizards to reveal the secret of the sinking foundations, and when they were silent he triumphantly disclosed the existence of a pool below, and in the pool a white dragon and a red were found sleeping. These monsters Geoffrey interpreted in the *Prophecies* as representing the Saxons and the Britons; and the Red Dragon has been the emblem of Wales ever since. Later, Merlin reappears as a mature man who by his contrivances transported the huge stones, now known as Stonehenge, from Ireland to Salisbury Plain as a monument to the Britons massacred by Hengist; and for this account Geoffrey may have drawn on a local tradition of great antiquity.

When Geoffrey came to write the *Life of Merlin* some fifteen years later, he had learned much more about the Welsh tradition, and the result is highly inconsistent with his early sketch of the mage; but he was not the kind of man to be greatly concerned. The prophet has now become King of South Wales, and allying himself with other kings fights *against* Guennolous (Gwennddolau), who has become King of Scotland. Crazed with grief at the loss of three brothers, Merlin retires to the wood of Caledon and fills it with his laments. Twice he is brought in bonds to the court of Rodarchus (Rhydderch). Geoffrey took advantage of these occasions to introduce the motif of the three mysterious laughs, which, originating in India, had been caught up into the Lailoken legend. Merlin laughs when he observes Rodarchus pluck a leaf from the Queen's hair, unwitting that it gave proof of her rendezvous with a lover; he laughs again when he sees a beggar and knows that he is sitting over buried treasure; he laughs a third time when he beholds a young man buying new shoes, unaware that he is shortly to be drowned. The Welsh poetic tradition is reflected in a long discourse of Taliesin, but the subject matter is drawn from the Encyclopedia of Isidore. The 'prophecies' here attributed to Merlin deal with calamities which happened to the Britons before Geoffrey's time. Oddly enough, in all this miscellany Arthur never appears associated with the prophet. It was through the *History of the Kings of Britain*, and the prophecies included in it, that Merlin achieved his prodigious reputation.

But Robert de Boron, whose crude poem on Joseph of Arimathea we examined in the previous chapter, also made a contribution to Merlin's fame, not so much by means of his own poem as through the prose redaction. His *Merlin* survives only as a fragment and must have had a very limited circulation. Though in the main it follows Wace's account of Merlin, it makes some very notable, imaginative additions. The first is the opening scene where the demons, infuriated by Christ's descent into hell and his leading away the righteous Jews, hold council and decide to bring about the ruin of mankind by the engendering of a false prophet, half human, half devil. A fiend, assigned to the task, succeeds in copulating with a pious virgin in her sleep, but the offspring, though hairy in body, does not inherit his father's malign nature, and, being promptly baptized, devotes his supernatural wisdom to good ends. The first exploit of the precocious babe is to defend his mother against the charge of incontinence, and, when the judge seems incredulous, to produce evidence that the judge himself is a bastard. Abruptly the clock is set forward from the first to the fifth century, and we get a distorted account of the reigns of the British kings preceding Arthur. The episodes of Vortigern's tower and the erection of Stonehenge are re-told, with variations, from Wace. A striking novelty is Merlin's display of puckish humour, amusing himself and mystifying King Uther and his messengers by assuming different forms. Now he is a woodcutter with a long beard, bristly hair, and an axe; now a herdsman; now a handsome youth.

But the two most striking additions to Wace's narrative are the development of the Round Table theme and the choice of Arthur by the sword in the stone. The table, according to Robert de Boron, was not made for Arthur as in Wace and Layamon, but for Uther: it was not made to betoken equality but to symbolize the Holy Trinity, for it was a replica of the table of the Grail fashioned by Joseph of Arimathea, which in turn was a replica of the table of the Last Supper. Thus the triad of tables served to bring into unity the fellowship of the apostles, the fellowship of Joseph's disciples, and, by anticipation, the fellowship of Arthur's knights. The climax of Robert's poem is well known at third and fourth hand through Malory and Tennyson. The birth of Arthur was under a shadow; was he Uther's legitimate son and rightful heir? Merlin took the situation in hand. Before the cathedral at London a block of marble was placed; fixed in the block was an anvil, and in the anvil was wedged a sword. An inscription designated as the rightful King of England him who could free the brand. All the knights and barons of the realm pull at it in vain. Suspense mounts. By pure chance, Arthur, a mere boy, performs the feat. Merlin's wisdom is proved once more, and Arthur, after some delay, mounts the throne.

There can be little doubt that, whether due to lost sources or not, Robert's *Merlin* is far superior to his *Joseph*.

The continuator, who after 1230 stretched the *Vulgate Merlin* to something over four hundred and sixty folio pages, was fully aware of the grandiose scheme of the Vulgate cycle, of which the *History of the Holy Grail*, the *Lancelot*, the *Quest*, and the *Mort Artu* were already in his hands. Accordingly, there are references backwards and forwards. Ban and Bors are brought in from the *Lancelot* to serve as allies to Arthur; Pelles and his daughter are introduced from the same source, and the birth of Galahad is prognosticated. An episode is invented to explain how Gawain came into the possession of his famous steed Gringalet.

To fill the vast expanse of parchment, the author searched out some hoary old themes. Arthur's fight with the monster cat of Lausanne is without doubt an echo of Kai's fight with the Cath Paluc mentioned in Chapter 1. The war between Arthur and his rebel brother-in-law, King Lot, since it seems to be cognate with his later wars with Lucius and Lancelot, is probably traditional. The motif of the enchanted carole, the circle of dancers who cannot break away, still survives in Welsh folklore. But a large proportion of the space is filled with detailed accounts of combats, battles, sieges, and if there is a tournament it turns into a fight. One might suspect that the author was a retired British soldier, for he never seems to weary of vicariously dismembering Saxon warriors. Of course, he was a French cleric, but there is no religious fervour in his work, and he evinces a marked interest in scandal. King Leodegan, Arthur's father-in-law, begets two daughters on the same night, the second on the wife of his seneschal. The good King Ban is also a faithless husband. Arthur produces three illegitimate sons, one of them, Modred, by incestuous union with his sister. This Arthur is someone very different from Tennyson's 'blameless king'.

The most successful episodes in the Merlin continuation of the Vulgate cycle are, appropriately enough, those concerned with the enchanter himself. He remains the guiding genius of Arthur's reign. He bears in battle the fire-spitting dragon standard. He gallops through the streets of Rome and into Julius Caesar's palace in the form of a stag, turns himself into a black, shaggy wild man, allows himself to be captured, and finally reveals to the astonished Caesar that his wife is an adulteress and that her twelve ladies-in-waiting are pages disguised in feminine attire—Oriental *fabliau* material. Offsetting this hardly edifying mission to Rome is a voyage to Jerusalem, where Merlin interprets the dream of a Saracen king as prognosticating the conversion of the monarch and his people to Christianity.

And running through a large part of the *Merlin* continuation is the story of the sage's infatuation with Niniane (Malory's

Nimue, Tennyson's Vivien). It had already been told in the *Lancelot*, but the new version is an improvement. The first meeting took place when Merlin in the guise of a handsome squire came upon the twelve-year-old damsel beside a clear spring. He satisfied her curiosity about his magic powers by producing visions of dancing knights and ladies, of a charming garden, of jongleurs singing. Smitten with love, he consents to give her lessons in magic, but she saves herself from his over-amorous embraces by placing a magic pillow in his lap. At last, when she has learned all his secrets, she decides to hold him in her power for ever. He keeps tryst with her in the Forest of Broceliande, and there under a flowering white-thorn she weaves a spell which puts her aged lover to sleep. When he wakes he fancies himself in the fairest tower in the world, and there Niniane dwells with him, submitting to his desires at last. No one ever saw the mage again, but Gawain, happening to pass by, heard his voice and learned of his betrayal.

This story of a wizard beguiled by a woman bears a vague analogy to current medieval fables about Aristotle and Virgil, and a much more specific likeness to Arthurian fays who imprison their lovers. But the author of this version has given the traditional theme a particularly felicitous shape. It is no small feat to have put a spell on both Tennyson and Matthew Arnold, and to have inspired the following lines from *Tristram and Iseult*:

> They sate them down together, and a sleep
> Fell upon Merlin, more like death, so deep.
> Her finger on her lips, then Vivian rose,
> And from her brown-lock'd head the wimple throws,
> And takes in her hand, and waves it over
> The blossom'd thorn-tree and her sleeping lover.
> Nine times she waved the fluttering wimple round,
> And made a little plot of magic ground.
> And in that daisied circle, as men say,
> Is Merlin prisoner till the judgment-day.

THE RIMED ENGLISH ROMANCES

ARTHURIAN romance came to England not directly from the west, from Wales, but by the back door, as it were, from the south and the east, from Brittany and France. As we saw in Chapter 2, it came as a result of the Norman Conquest, with the influx of Breton lords and their entertainers, the *'fabulosi Britones'*. Like the Continental French, the Anglo-French were enchanted by tales of faery loves, magic talismans, tournaments, and combats with giants. Two Arthurian lais composed in Anglo-French have come down to us from the second half of the twelfth century, the farcical *Lai of the Horn* by Robert Biket and the romantic *Lanval* by Marie de France. The former relates with coarse gusto how a drinking horn, made by a malicious fay, was brought to Caerleon to test the virtue of the ladies of Arthur's court. When the King tries to drink from it he is drenched with wine, and would have killed the Queen for making him a cuckold. But his knights intervene, and when they in turn are disillusioned about the chastity of their wives Arthur is comforted and pardons his spouse. Garadue (Caradoc) alone passes the test, and is rewarded for his wife's virtue by the lordship of Cirencester.

Lanval is a clever piece of narrative art. The hero, poor and out of favour with Arthur, is wooed by a fay, who has left her land for his sake. She grants him her love and promises him great riches on condition that he keep the affair a secret. In his new prosperity he attracts the attention of the Queen, and when he rebuffs her she plays the part of Potiphar's wife. In order to prove his innocence he rashly boasts that he possesses a mistress more beautiful than the Queen. But his word does not suffice and he is condemned to death unless he can produce his lady, and she, since he has broken the taboo, has ceased to visit him. He awaits in despair the final judgment. Two maidens, clothed in cendal, ride in before the assembled court and announce the coming of their mistress. They make an impression by their beauty, but Lanval does not recognize them. King Arthur impatiently calls for judgment. The suspense mounts. Two damsels, even more splendidly clad, approach, but again Lanval is obliged to deny knowledge of them. Arthur demands an immediate verdict against him. At last a solitary rider of dazzling beauty, mounted on a white palfrey, clad in white with a purple mantle folded about her, comes and dismounts before the King and declares her love for Lanval. Thus he is exonerated. As she is about to ride away, he leaps from the mounting block on to her palfrey, and the two depart together to the Isle of Avalon.

The Celticity of the two lais is easily recognized. Garadue, better known as Caradoc, was a historic Welsh chief of the sixth century, also famed in Brittany, and a Welsh triad attests the reputation of his wife for unblemished chastity. Lanval's name is Breton, and his fairy-mistress who imposes on him a taboo of secrecy has a prototype in the Irish goddess Macha. But it is the delicate, sure touch of the Anglo-Norman poetess which has moulded the traditional matter into a shape of exquisite grace.

Besides the two surviving Anglo-French lais with Arthurian backgrounds, there must have been longer Arthurian romances in Anglo-French; and, in fact, two have come down to us in translation: first, *Lanzelet*, written by the Swiss priest, Ulrich von Zatzikhoven, in the last decade of the twelfth century, on the basis of a manuscript brought to Germany by an Anglo-French baron, Hugh de Morville; second, Malory's Book of Gareth. The former has already been mentioned in Chapter 4, and the latter will be treated as an example of Malory's talents in Chapter 12. The Anglo-French originals of both were typical composites of traditional material, the *Lanzelet* containing several elements from the biography of the Irish god Lugh, as well as a Welsh version of the abduction of

Guenevere; the latter drawing on sagas about Cuchulainn the son of Lugh, his rescue of Fand from her enemies, and his encounter with an axe-bearing giant with a replaceable head. Just as we have discerned a contrast between the coarse art of the *Lai of the Horn* and the delicate charm of *Lanval*, so, too, there is a contrast between the loose structure and the casual morality of *Lanzelet*, on the one hand, and the artistic design and the chivalric idealism of the Book of Gareth, on the other. But in all four of the narratives there is the same ebullient vitality, the same zest for adventure.

While lais and romances such as these were being composed in England for the French-speaking lords and ladies, there were humbler and less talented entertainers who catered to the classes who knew no French, minstrels who added to their old repertoire of tales about the Anglo-Saxon hero Wade and Havelok the Dane some of the newly fashionable stories about King Arthur and the knights of his court. But it was not until these English-speaking classes became more literate and prosperous that they created a considerable demand for written records of the romances which pleased them. By this time, say about the year 1300, the favourite heroes of an older generation had gone out of fashion and had been replaced by Richard Cœur de Lion, Alexander the Great, Guy of Warwick, and by the knights of the Table Round.

From the two centuries between 1300 and 1500 about sixteen Middle English Arthurian romances in rimed or alliterative verse have come down to us, ranging widely in quality from sheer doggerel to such masterpieces as Chaucer's Tale of the Wife of Bath and *Gawain and the Green Knight*. Two sweeping generalizations may be made about them. All had forerunners in French. All, or nearly all, were intended for recitation by minstrels or for reading aloud. Frequently the opening lines contain an appeal for silence. *Gawain and the Green Knight* offers an example:

> If ye will listen to this lai but a little while,
> I shall tell it at once as I heard it in town.

Sir Percyvell of Galles concludes:

> Now Jesus Christ, Heaven's King,
> As He is lord of all thing,
> Grant us all His blessing!
> Amen, for charity!

A convenient classification of these poems, and a significant one, may be based on the verse-form: 1, those written in tail-rime stanzas, like the one just quoted, or other combinations of long and short lines; 2, those composed in rimed couplets; 3, those written in alliterative lines, sometimes combined with rime. Each of these classes has its own distinctive features, apart from the versification.

The tail-rime stanza, originally derived from the French lyric, was a favourite with minstrels, who memorized the lines and recited them with a jaunty rhythm in the marketplace, the tavern, or the baronial hall. Their audiences, we may infer, cared little for atmospheric effect, refined sentiment, or subtle psychology. Swift action and plenty of it was what they wanted, and what they got.

Typical are four poems combining long and short lines in stanzas, and dealing with the Matter of Britain, which were once included in a famous anthology, though three of them were torn out and are known only from other copies. Now called the Auchinleck manuscript, it was written by five scribes in a London book-dealer's shop about 1330. Each of the four pieces is a derivative from or a cognate of a French poem. *Sir Tristrem* is a condensed version of Thomas's *Tristan*; *Sir Launfal* is derived at two removes from Marie de France's *Lanval*; *Libeaus Desconus* is a free re-telling of *Le Bel Inconnu* (*The Handsome Unknown*); *Sir Percyvell of Galles* corresponds roughly to the first part of Chrétien's *Perceval*, but cannot be derived from it, for it preserves at least two features of the ultimate Irish source—the hero's speed of foot and his obligation to avenge his father's death—which the French poem lacks, and there is no hint of the Grail theme. To a greater or less degree,

all four poems are marred by stereotyped phrases and meaningless fillers, such as 'without fable', 'it is not to lain [hide]'.
But since the English minstrel or hack shared these failings
with Homer and Chaucer, we should not judge him too
severely.

And in spite of their defects the four poems are of considerable interest to the literary historian. The worst of the lot is
Sir Tristrem, but the author attempted the impossible—to tell
the great love-story in short compass and in a stanza with the
very difficult rime-scheme, abababab*c*bc, in which *c* consists
of only two or three syllables. The result is doggerel and must
often have been unintelligible to the hearers. An amusing
point is the rimester's claim to have been at Erceldoun (in
southern Scotland) and to have heard the poem recited by a
certain Thomas, presumably the Thomas of Erceldoun who
was famous as a prophet in the second half of the thirteenth
century. Here Thomas, the Anglo-French author of *Tristan*,
whom our rimester followed but could never have heard, has
been deliberately confused with the prophet. *Sir Launfal*, because
of its dependence on *Lanval*, retains a little of the dramatic
appeal and elfin charm of its original, but since these were
not enough for his prospective audience the author added the
excitement of a tournament at Caerleon and a duel on horseback in Lombardy.

He also composed *Libeaus Desconus*, a romance of special
interest because we know so much of its history. The first part,
which is closely related to *Le Bel Inconnu* and Malory's tale of
Gareth and Lynet, had its ultimate source in a famous Irish
saga, *The Wasting Sickness of Cuchulainn*. Just as the damsel
Elene came to the court of King Arthur to seek a champion for
her mistress against her enemies, and Gingelein returned with
her to accomplish that mission, so Liban came to the court of
Ulster, to seek aid for her sister Fand against her enemies, and
Cuchulainn returned with her and fufilled that mission. The
dragon-maiden who was transformed by a kiss into a ravishing
beauty goes back to the Irish tales of the monstrous hag transformed by union with the destined King of Ireland—tales to be

discussed later in this chapter. The setting of this metamorphosis in the ruined city of Sinadoun belongs to a much later stage when the ruins of the Roman fort of Segontium were called 'the city of Snowdon' and were thought to be haunted.

The Middle English romance has lost much of the glamorous supernaturalism of its French source, such as the nightmarish illusions with which the fay of the Ille d'Or torments Guinglain. The result is that we are left with an assortment of physical combats with knights, giants, and magicians. Added to monotony is naiveté. When Gingelein presented the heads of two giants to Elene, the maid was glad and blithe and thanked God many times that ever he was made a knight. However, the poem found an admirer even in the eighteenth century. Bishop Percy, editor of the *Reliques of Ancient English Poetry*, commended it as showing 'how nature and common sense had supplied to these old simple bards the want of critical art and taught them some of the most essential rules of Epic Poetry'.

The author of *Libeaus Desconus* may have been old and simple in some ways, but he was no bard with haggard eyes and hoary hair, streaming like a meteor, such as Thomas Gray depicted, but a London hack and an accomplished, though blameless, plagiarist. A very intricate piece of detective work by Laura Hibbard Loomis has demonstrated that the romances contained in the Auchinleck manuscript were largely the result of collaborative effort under the direction of the book-dealer, or publisher, as we would call him today. In *Libeaus* we find correspondences to phrases and sequences of detail in *Sir Tristrem*, *Sir Launfal*, *Guy of Warwick*, *Bevis of Hampton*, *Sir Degaré*, and *Roland and Vernagu*—correspondences so exact as to rule out the possibility of mere coincidence. For example:

Libeaus	*Bevis*
His berd was yelow as wax,	His berd was yelw, to is brest
To his gerdell heng his fax	wex
[hair]	And to his gerdel heng is fax

Libeaus	*Degaré*
His scheld was asur fin,	With the scheld of asur
Thre bores heddes ther inne.	And thre bor hevedes ther in,
	Wel ipainted with gold fin.

All six romances which show these correspondences with *Libeaus* are, or were, contained in the Auchinleck manuscript. There can be only one explanation. *Libeaus* was composed in a commercial scriptorium where these texts were available, and, though indebted for its narrative outline to the French *Le Bel Inconnu*, it is actually in the details of its expression a cento of cribs from the six Middle English poems. The literary hack who performed this feat was not trying to deceive anyone; there were no copyright laws, and little sense of literary property. His composite poem must have suited popular taste, for six copies survive, including the famous Percy Folio.

Best of the Arthurian pieces once contained in the Auchinleck manuscript is *Sir Percyvell of Galles*. It was not the product of a London hack, but was composed in the north. Its dialect recalls that of the students in Chaucer's Reeve's Tale, who came from Northumberland. About six-sevenths of the poem is matched by similar episodes in Chrétien's *Perceval*, and for reasons stated above may be regarded as a remote cognate. One misses in it the French refinement of style and the tantalizing mystery of the Grail theme, of which there is not a trace. But in clarity of motivation and coherence of plot the English poem is superior. Percyvell fulfils the three obligations incumbent on him: he avenges his father's murder by killing the Red Knight; he marries his ladylove; he finds his grief-stricken mother and restores her to health and sanity. And whereas Chrétien's hero drops out of the story Sir Percyvell dies fighting nobly in the Holy Land.

The comic theme of Perceval's blundering behaviour as an innocent abroad, so cleverly developed by Chrétien, is handled with equal zest by the anonymous English poet, and we are given some added instances of the 'child's' naiveté. His mother charges him on his departure to be 'of mesure', that is, to exercise moderation. When, shortly afterward, he enters a mansion and finds provision for man and beast, he dutifully divides it all into two equal measures, leaves one half alone and with the other feeds himself and his mare. 'How could he be of greater measure?' comments the poet. Still later, having exchanged the mare for a steed, the boy is so ignorant of sex that he still thinks he is riding a mare; so, when he is in the midst of a combat with a giant named Gollerothiram, he is so puzzled by Gawain's telling him to dismount from his 'steed' and fight on foot, that he barely recovers from his bewilderment in time to avoid a fatal blow. *Sir Percyvell* is not high art, but it offers us a well-knit plot, plenty of rough-and-tumble fighting, and honest fun.

The same scholar who was able to trace the Auchinleck manuscript to the activities of a commercial scriptorium in London proved conclusively that it was this very volume which came into the hands of a London poet and inspired one of the most brilliant parodies in literature, *Sir Thopas*. How do we know that it was precisely this manuscript and no other which excited Chaucer's risible muscles? It has long been realized that the tail-rime stanza tune and its variations were among the butts of his ridicule, and that he echoed phrases from romances in the Auchinleck manuscript. The evidence that he must have had the book in his hands is complex, and so two obvious borrowings must serve in place of many. In the manuscript Chaucer would have read: 'If thou wilt truly to me take and all women for me forsake.' He wrote, as surrogate for Thopas: 'All other women I forsake and to an elf-queen I me take.' And if we cast back to the passage quoted above from *Libeaus*, need we ask where Chaucer got the mocking description of the carpet knight: 'His heer [hair], his berd was lyk saffroun, that to his girdel raughte [reached] adoun'?

It should be emphasized that he was making fun, not of the whole body of chivalric romance, but of the popular minstrel type, somewhat commercialized in the Auchinleck manuscript, and that he exaggerated its defects. Of course, he had as much right to do so as Fielding had to expose in *Tom*

Thumb the Great the rhetorical absurdities of heroic tragedy, or as W. S. Gilbert had to burlesque the conventions of Italian opera and British melodrama. But parody is not always fair; in *Libeaus* the yellow beard, reaching to the girdle, belonged not to the hero but, much more appropriately, to the grotesque figure of his dwarf. The tail-rime romances, though they afford an essential key to the wit of *Sir Thopas*, afford also good entertainment in themselves.

Let us pass from these to what is known as the *Stanzaic Morte Arthur*, to be distinguished from the *Alliterative Morte Arthur*, discussed in the next chapter. It employs, with occasional variations, the rime-scheme abababab, without cauda. It is assigned to the late fourteenth century and to the north-west Midlands. Its author had a limited and stereotyped vocabulary, and the difficulty of finding so many rime-words forced him to use meaningless or awkward line-fillers. What could be more banal than the description of the Maid of Astolat? 'Her rode [complexion] was red as blossom on briar, or flower that springeth in the field.' And it does not surprise one that Guenevere also is 'bright as blossom on briar'. The stoutest knights of the Round Table swoon as readily as the heroines of an eighteenth-century novel.

But the poet was not altogether artless. A comparison with his source, the *Vulgate Mort Artu*, shows that he exercised taste and intelligence in the process of condensation. Though many of his changes seem to be due to imperfect memory, others represent omission of unessentials and the linking up of scattered elements in order to produce a more continuous narrative. Moreover, in the stark simplicity of certain passages there is strength. While Arthur is away hunting, Lancelot seeks the Queen's chamber and is accused by her of an intrigue with the Maid of Astolat.

> Lancelot full still there stood,
> His heart was heavy as any stone. . . .
> 'Madam,' he said, 'for Cross and Rood,
> What betokeneth all this moan?

> By Him that bought me with His blood,
> Of these tidings know I none.
>
> 'But by these tidings it seemeth me
> Away ye would that I were.
> Now have good day, my lady free,
> For sooth, thou seest me never mair.'
> Out of the chamber then wends he;
> Now ask if his heart was full of care!

As the critics have already noted, the whole tragedy of the *Morte d'Arthur* is summed up in the comment of the knights:

> 'Alas,' they said, 'Lancelot du Lake,
> That ever shouldst thou see the Queen!'

Apart from these instrinsic merits, the *Stanzaic Morte Arthur* possesses historic importance, for Malory's *Morte d'Arthur*, published in 1485, reveals its influence on some of the classic passages of the last two books. This influence will be treated in some detail in the chapter on Malory. Through Malory it extended itself to the best of the *Idylls of the King*, the *Passing of Arthur*.

We come at last to a poem, *Ywain and Gawain*, which reveals the influence of a French model not only on the content but also on the verse-form, for it follows faithfully the narrative outline of Chrétien's masterpiece *Ivain*, and employs the same octosyllabic riming couplet. Though composed in the north, like *Sir Percyvell*, and beginning with a minstrel invocation of a blessing on those who hearken to *Ywain and Gawain*, it is comparatively free from the crudities of the minstrel style. In fact, one may suspect that it was no rimester of the marketplace or the village green, but a schoolmaster or a priest who composed this excellent adaptation from the French, with its very pious beginning and conclusion. At any rate, the shafts of ridicule which Chaucer directed against the tail-rime romances leave the smooth, polished surface of this poem undented.

Chrétien's six thousand eight hundred lines are reduced to approximately four thousand—a reduction effected largely by abbreviating the analyses of sentiment. It is quite unnecessary to see in the grateful lion 'a symbol of the courage which Ywain finds in himself' (an extreme example of the symbolistic mania) in order to enjoy the animal's very human and humorous behaviour. Lunet is just as wily as Chrétien's Lunete, and the English poet seems to have enjoyed the piquant scene where she persuaded her mistress, Alundine, to get down on her knees and take an oath on relics, a chalice, and a missal—Chrétien has only a single relic—to do all in her power to reconcile the Knight of the Lion with his lady, Alundine not knowing that the Knight of the Lion was her own husband.

It may be heresy to say so, but I say it unblushingly: *Ywain and Gawain* is a better story, better told, than most of the stories in Gower's *Confessio Amantis* and than several of the *Canterbury Tales*. It is a better romance that the Wife of Bath's Tale, for there can be little chivalrous feeling in a narrative of which the hero, though a knight of Arthur's fellowship, is a rapist. Considered, however, as a *fabliau* and as a revelation of the teller's robust, humorous, masterful, and voluptuous nature, the tale of the Wife is one of Chaucer's great successes. First, a brief résumé of the plot.

A young unnamed knight of Arthur's household was guilty of violating a maiden, was accused by the victim before King Arthur, and sentenced to death. But at the Queen's request he was given the respite of twelve months and a day, and was offered his life if before the expiration of that time he could answer the question: What do women most crave? He went about asking every woman he met, but received such a variety of answers that he was in despair. On the last day he spied on the edge of a forest more than four and twenty ladies dancing, who as he approached vanished. But in their place an ugly old crone was sitting on the green. Told of his predicament, she whispered the secret in his ear, but only on condition that he fulfil the first request she made of him. When the knight announced before the Queen and her ladies that women desire above everything else sovereignty over their lovers and husbands, no lady challenged his answer and his life was spared, but the crone demanded that he keep his bargain and marry her. On the nuptial night he lay beside his wife, writhing in agony. She offered him a choice between having her ugly and true and having her beautiful and faithless. After reflection he left the choice to her; and thereupon, having achieved dominion over him, she rewarded him by promising to be both fair and true.

This is, of course, a tale of faerie, and it has two English variants, a romance and a ballad, of which the hero is Gawain. Other Arthurian versions substitute a dragon-woman for the ugly crone, omit the motif of choice, and make the transformation dependent on a kiss. All this association with Arthur's court, the attachment to Arthurian heroes (Gawain, Lanzelet, Guinglain), and the supernatural machinery of vanishings and metamorphoses, establish a strong probability that the stories of the transformed hag were of Celtic origin. As long ago as 1892 Stokes pointed out a group of Irish stories as the likeliest source of the Wife of Bath's Tale. The earliest version, a poem entitled the *Adventures of the Sons of Eochaid Mugmedon*, was composed by a poet who died in 1024, and tells how the historical King of Ireland, Niall of the Nine Hostages, proved his right to the sovereignty. In his youth he was sent with his four half-brothers, as a test of valour, on a hunt. Each of the five in turn approached a spring, and each was faced by a repulsive old woman, who demanded a kiss. Four of them turned away in horror. But Niall not only kissed her but also cohabited with her, whereupon she was transfigured into a radiant beauty. She declared herself to be the Sovereignty of Ireland, and explained that as she was ugly at first, so was the kingship difficult to obtain. By his display of courage, Niall earned the royal title.

Here, obviously, the loathly hag is an allegorical figure, personifying the rulership of Ireland. But there is ample evidence that at an earlier stage she was a goddess, Eriu,

personifying Ireland itself, and that the account of her metamorphosis was a Nature myth explaining the miracle of spring.
Before her transformation, blacker was her face than any
visage; larger than a rock in a wall was each of her rough black
knees; a rugged hilly thick black head was on her, like a furzy
mountain. Another text describes her after the change, thus:
'Blooming her countenance in hue as the crimson lichen of
Leinster crags . . . her locks were like Bregon's buttercups; a
mantle about her, matchless, green.' Thus Eriu glows in the
imagination with the magic of poetry and Niall takes on the
vitalizing powers of the sun.

It is a long way from this myth by way of political allegory
and romance of faerie to the semi-dramatic self-revealing tale
of the Wife of Bath; and some may question this development
since nothing is left of the Nature myth but the transformation
motif, and little is left of the allegory except the struggle for
sovereignty, changed in meaning from kingship to marital
domination. But given the strong antecedent probability in
favour of such an origin, it is not too much to believe that,
when the concept of political rule as an ugly woman became
obscure, a clever story-teller substituted the concept of
sovereignty in marriage and the dominant female. Other
critics may dismiss the matter of origins as irrelevant, and
they are right to the extent that Chaucer knew nothing of
Irish mythology, and the modern reader may relish his re-
interpretation of the theme without ever reading an Irish saga.
But I cannot help thinking that the poet himself, with his avid
interest in mythology, would have been fascinated by the prehistory of his tale; and so, I think, are most students of letters
who are interested in the workings of the imagination as
revealed not merely in masterpieces but also in its humbler
manifestations.

Turning our attention to the masterpiece itself, we may all
agree that the Wife of Bath's Tale possesses the attractions of
three types of medieval fiction. There is the elfin charm of a
Breton lai in the vision of the fairy dance and the mysterious
appearance of the hideous crone in their place. There is the

dubbio, or problem-tale, calculated to stir debate, and in this regard there can be no doubt of the Wife's success. There is something, too, of the cynicism and prurient interest of the *fabliau* inasmuch as the hero, though guilty of a crime against womanhood, is finally pardoned by a court of ladies, and the scene in which he lies, tossing and turning, beside his repulsive bride has its salacious undertones.

But the chief fascination of the tale for the general reader, as well as for the student, lies in the self-revelation of the teller. In a long prologue which Chaucer, we know, worked over with great care, adding new inspirations as they came to him, he achieved one of the most complex and living portraits in literature. Brazenly, boastfully, the old Wife exhibits to the pilgrims her lust, her deceitfulness, her shrewish eloquence, her domineering temper. Wistfully she looks back to the lost raptures of youth. Gleefully she recalls her triumphs over her five deceased husbands, especially over the fifth, a recalcitrant young cleric, from whom she had acquired some scraps of learning. Now, as a merry widow, she is ready to welcome a sixth. As she was about to begin her tale, the Friar interrupted with the sneering remark: 'Now, dame, this is a long preamble of a tale'—a remark which she does not forget.

We know that Chaucer intended at first to assign to the Wife the tale which later he assigned to the Shipman—a *fabliau* about the gullibility of husbands and most unlikely to attract a sixth for the teller. Luckily he discovered the story of the Hag Transformed, realized its appropriateness to the dominating female in his company of pilgrims, and proceeded to make it dramatically suitable in the framework of the *Canterbury Tales*.

So, when the Host asks the Wife to begin her contribution to the series, she consents, adding with mock submissiveness: 'if I have leave of this worthy friar'. After a reference to the bygone days when Britain was filled with fairies, she explains their disappearance in deceptively serious fashion by the efficacy of the exorcisms practised by the friars, so that women may safely walk the roads. No incubus lurks under bush or tree, except the limitour himself. This is surely the same clever woman who has just been bragging of her ability to cow her husbands with her tongue.

Chaucer next adapts the Wife's tale to the teller by introducing as the hero a knight guilty of rape (as in no other version) and by representing the Queen and her ladies as eager to save the life of so venial an offender. The condition on which he is promised a full pardon is not of Chaucer's invention, but it gives the Wife a welcome opportunity to list and comment on the various objects of women's desire. She dismisses the wish for secrecy as absurd, and tells Ovid's story of King Midas and his ears, substituting, however, the King's wife for his barber, and concluding: 'Here may ye see, though we a time abide, Yet out it must; we can no counsel hide.'

A very significant departure from tradition is the absence of repulsive details in the description of the hag—details in which other versions of her story luxuriated. Why this omission? It has been suggested—and rightly, I believe—that the Wife identifies herself with the hag; though she recognizes that she is no longer young and beautiful, she will not conceive herself as a monster of ugliness.

When we come to the long curtain-lecture which the hag delivers to her unwilling husband on the wedding night, Chaucer seems for once to forget who is supposed to be talking. It is natural enough for the hag, and for the Wife of Bath who speaks through her, to be sensitive about their humble birth and their age; it is plausible enough for the Wife, lately married to a clerk, to offer two or three quotations in support of her views. But a discourse citing Dante, Valerius Maximus, Tullius Hostilius, Boethius, and Seneca could never have been uttered by the cloth-maker of Bath, even less by the hag. The poet, of course, was well aware of the incongruity. Why did he let the learned lecture stand? I can think of no other reason than that he felt passionately on the subject of true gentility—in fact, he composed a ballade on the topic—and so sacrificed dramatic propriety to personal feeling. It is Geoffrey Chaucer who speaks, not Alice of Bath.

This lapse is more than redeemed by the clever change which the poet made in the alternatives offered by the hag to her unhappy knight, namely, to have her fair and faithless, or ugly and true. For this is a realistic alternative, one which many a man has faced in the choice of a wife. The traditional alternative, presented by three versions, namely, whether the hag should be hideous by day and fair by night, or vice versa, was a pleasant fairy-tale fantasy, but would not do for the hard-headed Wife of Bath and her creator.

When the knight relinquished his masculine prerogative of decision as between the alternatives, the hag exclaimed— and we can hear with what a whoop of triumph the Wife of Bath interpreted the lines: 'Then have I got of you "maistrie" since I may choose and govern as I please?' So the hag, who was really the Queen of the Fairies, achieved what women most crave, and graciously promised to be both fair and faithful. Drawing aside the bed-curtain, the startled husband found the first part of the promise already realized. Beside him lay a damsel matching in loveliness any empress or queen. Cheerful and challenging, the Wife concludes with a prayer to Christ to send women husbands, meek, young, and fresh abed, and with another prayer to cut short the lives of niggardly and obstinate spouses. Whether she picked up a sixth husband on the strength of her revelatory effusion, Chaucer does not say, but that she kept the pilgrims spellbound, as she has held vaster audiences since, there can be no manner of doubt.

II

THE ALLITERATIVE ENGLISH
ROMANCES

The English alliterative romances differ from the others not only as to metrical form but also in vocabulary and geographical origin; two of them, the *Alliterative Morte Arthur* and *Gawain and the Green Knight*, reflect a more aristocratic culture and a more sophisticated technique than any of the tail-rime poems. Though both begin with an address to the listeners, no one would dream that they were the products of itinerant minstrels. They are among the most brilliant examples of what is generally called the Alliterative Revival, though it might be termed more accurately the Alliterative Survival, since it refers to the continuation into the sixteenth century of the old Anglo-Saxon traditions of verse.

There is no reason to believe that the tradition of alliterative poetry, though it seemed to be breaking down in Layamon's *Brut*, died out in the hundred and fifty years following, and then was resurrected in the middle of the fourteenth century. Far from it. Only a flourishing oral transmission can account for the richness of the poetic vocabulary and the standardization of the metrics exhibited by such a poem as the *Alliterative Morte Arthur*. In districts removed from the dominant French influence, people of English and Scandinavian descent and of various social ranks must have listened, rapt, to poets chanting narratives in the manner of their ancestors. But these auditors were not wealthy and literate enough to employ scribes to write down the effusions of the poets in this medium. Only with the rise of this element in literacy and affluence, and with the conversion of the

Anglo-French aristocracy to the use of English, exemplified by the commissioning of the Alliterative *William of Palerne* by Humphrey de Bohun, Earl of Hereford, in 1355, did the splendid but evanescent poetry of the provincial districts of the north and west attain permanence in manuscript form.

At the same time other factors were combining to weld the whole of England into unity. The wars with Scotland and France created a patriotism—and a jingoism—in which all parts of the country shared. In the early years of his reign Edward III made York his administrative centre, and thus contributed to the mingling of northerners and southerners. The sensational naval victories of Sluys and Winchelsea and the even more spectacular triumphs at Crecy and Poitiers rendered him popular with all classes. At the height of his fortunes he held both the King of France and the King of Scotland prisoner. No wonder that the chronicler, Jean le Bel, wrote: 'When the noble Edward first gained England in his youth, nobody thought much of the English, nobody spoke of their prowess and courage. . . . Now in the time of the noble Edward, who has often put them to the test, they are the finest and most daring warriors known to man.' Thus Edward was not only a sovereign but also a Nelson and a Wellington, and all Englishmen, save a minority who felt that the blood and treasure might better have been spent against the common foe of all Christians in the Mediterranean, took pride in every achievement of English arms.

England was prosperous. Loot and ransom money flowed in; wool flowed out but brought a good price. Once the terrific plague which ravaged Europe had died down in 1349, those who survived in England had 'never had it so good'. The victory over the Spanish fleet off Winchelsea took place in 1350, Poitiers in 1356. Who can help feeling in the *Alliterative Morte Arthur* the spirit of the fifties, and recognizing in its hero a strong resemblance to Edward, third of the Plantagenet line? It must have been in this period, before disillusionment set in, that the poem was composed by an ardent patriot of the upper class (cleric or secular), brought up in the north country. It is suggestive that he placed Arthur's court at Carlisle, and brought him by way of Catterick to York.

Probably the poet had taken part in Edward's warlike activities, or had received detailed reports from eyewitnesses, so vividly does he describe in terms of his own day the fabled operations of Arthur's time. In the great battle with the Emperor Lucius, located significantly in northern France, Arthur posted bowmen of Britain on the flanks, whose arrows pierced the fine mail of the Romans and crippled their steeds. We seem to be reading about Crecy. The foraging expedition sent out by Arthur during the siege of Metz must have had many parallels during Edward's campaigns, when his forces lived largely off the country. It has long been recognized that the account of the sea-battle with Modred's fleet is patterned closely after the English naval victory over a Spanish fleet in 1350—so closely that Modred's demoralized sailors who jumped overboard are referred to as Spaniards.

The main literary source of the *Alliterative Morte Arthur* is Geoffrey of Monmouth's *History*, but it serves merely as a framework to be filled out by the poet's imagination. With good judgment he begins with the claim for tribute from the Emperor Lucius, and continues with Arthur's scornful reply, the assembling of his army and the entrusting of his kingdom to Modred, the crossing to Barfleur, the killing single-handed of the giant of Mont St Michel, the victory over the Romans, Arthur himself ending the fray with a stroke which cleaves the Emperor's breast. There follows a long digression. Arthur invades Lorraine, besieges Metz, eventually takes it, and advances into Italy as far as Viterbo, the route from Lucerne over the St Gothard Pass being clearly indicated. After the ominous dream of Fortune's wheel the narrative returns to Geoffrey's outline. News comes of Modred's treason, Arthur crosses to Britain, Gawain dies in the landing, Modred flees to Cornwall, and there in the last battle he is killed and Arthur mortally wounded. Instead of being conveyed to the Isle of Avalon to be healed, he is brought to Glastonbury and there entombed.

The poem gives evidence of familiarity with several French works. Probably from the *Vulgate Mort Artu* came the dream of Fortune and her wheel. The listing of the Nine Worthies, conquerors who mounted or were destined to mount on the wheel, was taken from the *Vows of the Peacock*, a popular French offshoot of the Alexander cycle, written about 1312. From the same poem came the suggestion for the vows taken by King Aungers, the Baron of Little Britain, the King of Wales, Ewayn, and others, to perform specific exploits in the battle with Lucius. The *Foraging Expedition of Gadres*, another French Alexander romance, inspired the similar expedition in the alliterative poem, as is proved by the appearance of Floridas as a leader in both accounts. The duel between Gawain and Priamus, resulting in desperate wounds for both and the conversion of the latter, is a patent borrowing from *Fierabras* or some other Charlemagne epic.

Indeed, the *Morte Arthur* itself has been classed as an epic, and there is nothing about it peculiarly romantic—no love interest, no mystery. Like most of the *chansons de geste*, *Beowulf*, and the *Iliad*, it is preoccupied with deeds of physical prowess. There are long stretches devoted to thrusts of lance and cuts of sword, as exciting—or boring—as similar passages in the *Iliad* or a running commentary on a football match. By chance, the *Morte Arthur* and *Beowulf* offer a certain parallelism in depicting a fight with a monster and ending with the death and obsequies of a hero. A comparison is not favourable to the later poem. The shadowy figure of the nocturnal prowler Grendel, the haunted mere, the taut, swift narrative of the combat are more impressive than the later poet's picture of Arthur's ride through a wood full of roses and songbirds, his jest about seeking the 'saint' of Mont St Michel, and the description of the thirty-foot 'saint' himself, warming his bare buttocks by a fire, while maidens turn the spit on which morsels of christened children are being broiled. But in spite of such aberrations of taste, the *Alliterative Morte Arthur* possesses epic grandeur and the heroic mood. The *Beowulf* poet would not be ashamed of his successor.

The *Morte Arthur* is not, of course, dramatic in form, but its structure, though based on Geoffrey, is clearly that of tragedy. Arthur's star rises and sets. In the opening scene he holds high court, surrounded by prelates and princes, lords and ladies, from as far west as Ireland and as far east as Austria. His right and his power are challenged by the Emperor of Rome. In the course of the rising action he not only defeats and kills the Emperor, but even receives the offer of the imperial crown from the Pope. At this apex of his career Arthur has the pre-monitory dream of Fortune's wheel. Promptly follows the falling action, ending in the fatal battle with Modred. That the author was conscious of this symmetrical pattern is clear from his transposing the dream of Fortune from its position in the *Mort Artu*, the eve of the last battle, to the central point.

Recently an authority on the poem has argued that it is an *exemplum*, in which Arthur, exemplifying pride, is punished for his sin, and that, by implication, King Edward is the object of a stern rebuke. Is the poem, then, a pacifist tract? Modern historians may animadvert on the futility of the Hundred Years' War, and few today would deny that it left a calamitous heritage of hatred. But the poet made little or no critical comment. For him, as for Caspar in Southey's poem, 'it was a glorious victory', and that was enough. That his sympathies were entirely with Arthur—and by implication with Edward—comes out clearly in his selection of Arthur's adversaries. As in Geoffrey, many of them are Moslems, and he adds the heathens of Prussia and Lithuania and a batch of giants. So Arthur is not a pagan Alexander, dominated by pride and a lust for power, but a Christian like Charlemagne, fighting for his rights and for the faith. The tragic ending is due to no fault of his, no *hamartia*. Realistically considered, it is the result of Modred's unforeseeable treason; in terms of symbolism, it is the result of Lady Fortune's treachery.

She appears as a duchess, descending from the clouds, apparelled in silk, with yard-long 'lappets' attached to her sleeves, very fashionable in the fifties and sixties. Six kings clinging to her wheel of gold were one by one hurled to earth, and two others, trying to climb up on it, failed. She then lifted Arthur on to a seat mounted on the wheel, and presented him with a sceptre, diadem, orb, and sword.

> 'Then she went to the well   by the wood's edges,
> Which welled with wine   and wondrously flowed,
> Caught up a cupful   and covered it fairly.
> She bade me drink deeply   a draught to herself.
> Thus she led me about   for the length of an hour
> With all the love and goodwill   that one could desire.
> But at midday exactly   all her mood changed,
> And much she menaced me   with marvellous words.
> When I called for pity   she cast down her brows.
> "King, thou criest in vain,   by Christ who made me!
> For thou shalt lose this game   and thy life later;
> Thou hast lived long enough   in delight and lordship."
> About she whirled the wheel   and whirled me under,
> So that each bit of my body   was battered to pieces.'

Thus, though conventional religion prescribes the racial attitudes and the ceremonial acts, it is fatalism, personified by Fortune, which dominates the events—that fatalism which haunts English poetry from *Beowulf* to *The Dynasts*. Worked into this sombre scheme, this tragic pattern, are the variegated threads of violence, brutality, daring, chivalric honour, friendship, and grief.

All the best qualities of the *Morte Arthur* appear heightened in *Gawain and the Green Knight*—a rich vocabulary, clear visualization, shapely structure, vivacity, seriousness; and the worse features are absent—monotony, coarseness, chauvinism. When one discovers in the *Gawain* poem refinements of technique and subtleties of feeling, one is not likely to contest the verdict of critics that here is the masterpiece of medieval English romance. It combines the sturdiness of epic, the fantastic charm of romance, and the sophistication of a country-house novel.

It seems to have been written ten or twenty years later than the *Alliterative Morte Arthur*, as is suggested by the references to armour. The ailette, a shoulder-guard, has been discarded and the bacinet has been replaced by the helm, such as one sees over the Black Prince's monument at Canterbury, dated 1376. The linguists seem agreed that the dialect is that of Lancashire or an adjacent county. Nearly all scholars believe that the author composed three other poems preserved in the same manuscript: two narrative sermons based on Scripture, *Patience* and *Purity*, and an elegy in the form of a vision of a deceased maiden and of the heavenly Jerusalem, the *Pearl*. Especially strong is the evidence linking the last poem with *Gawain and the Green Knight*, but there is no clue to the author's name.

What, however, can we reasonably conjecture about him? He was not a priest and therefore not a chaplain in a noble household, but he might have been a secretary. In such a household he seems to belong, for he knew not only French secular literature but also courtly etiquette and the terminology of the chase. Was he perhaps the younger son of a noble, or even a noble himself, like Henry of Lancaster (father of Chaucer's Blanche the Duchess), who composed in French the pious *Livre de Seyntz Medicines*? Would he have attended lectures at Oxford or Cambridge and there picked up his knowledge of theological matters, evinced in the *Pearl*, and his use of legal terms?

Attempts to prove that the 'Master Anonymous' was somehow associated with an order of chivalry, which was distinguished by a green baldric, have been met with coldness, yet the feeling that there ought to be a link persists. Someone tacked on to the poem the motto of the Garter: '*Hony Soyt Qui Mal Pence*.' This was not helpful but rather confusing, since a blue garter on the left leg is something quite different from a green cincture worn over the right shoulder. Research has produced no record of an order whose insignia matched those which, in the poem, the knights of the Round Table adopted. We do know, however, that Edward III established in 1345 a fellowship of three hundred knights on the model of Arthur's, and then dropped the idea. Could it be that their badge was a green baldric? This is a mere guess, and even if correct would furnish little insight into the poet and the poem. What we can be sure of is that, however far his travels and his interests may have taken him, his heart was in the district whose language he spoke and among the friths and dales which he described so well.

The verse-form which he employed in *Purity* and *Patience* was the standard long alliterative line of the *Morte Arthur*, but in *Gawain and the Green Knight* he broke the monotony by dividing the poem into stanzas varying in length, each stanza ending with what is known as 'a bob and wheel'—five short lines, riming ababa. Usually this device serves as a kind of paragraph ending, and sometimes delivers what in theatrical lingo is called 'a punch line', as, for instance, when we are suddenly informed that the gigantic horseman who burst into Arthur's hall was coloured a deep-dyed green. The long lines provide opportunity for rhythmic and onomatopoetic effects, some of which can be reproduced in modern English. Listen as the Green Knight sharpens his axe.

What! it clattered in the cliff   as if it would cleave,
As if on a grindstone   one had ground a scythe.
What! it whirred and whetted   as water at a mill.

Listen to the stream:

The burn blubbered therein   as if it had boiled.

Feel the coming of spring:

Sheer sheds the rain   in showers full warm,
Falls on fair meadow-land;   flowers show forth.
Both the ground and the groves,   green are their robes.

The description of summer and autumn which comes after

conveys not only a wistful sense of time past, but also a fore-
boding of time to come, the dreaded rendezvous at the
Green Chapel. There is a subtle blend of verbal music and
emotional atmosphere; weather becomes poetry to a degree
which the conventional medieval poems of spring do not
attain.

Striking are the visual impressions. We ride with Gawain
as he approaches the castle of Sir Bercilak, first glimpsing it
from a distance as it shimmers and shines through bare oak
trees; then, as we reach the moat, we look down at the walls
descending into the water, and then turn our eyes upward to
the towers and pinnacles, and chalk-white chimneys, which,
outlined against the sky, seem as if cut out of paper, like the
decorations on a banquet table. In Arthur's hall we watch
spellbound as the huge knight, decapitated, picks up his head,
mounts his green steed, turns his bulk about, 'that ugly body
that bleeds', lifts up the head, and turns it towards the dais.

And it lifted up the eyelids   and looked staringly,
And spoke thus much with its mouth   as ye may now hear.

It is the perfection of plot in *Gawain and the Green Knight*
which is most surprising—a plot which brings into causal
relationship a complex of apparently disconnected facts;
which creates suspense and maintains it to the end; which
rounds out the action by bringing the hero back to the court
from which he had started. This impression of completion is
accentuated by the echoing of the opening lines in the concluding ones.

Was this plot original with the English poet? On this
question there is much difference of opinion. What is generally
agreed is that three distinct elements, each with its own history,
were brought together and skilfully intertwined. If a French
manuscript should turn up containing this same combination,
then the issue would be settled, and the French author would
be entitled to the credit—the great credit—of bringing unity
and plausibility out of three quite unrelated tales. Until this

happens, or until the *Gawain*-poet can be recalled from the dead, we shall not know precisely what he had to work with. Much, of course, is his own. No Frenchman is likely to have heard of Anglesey or the wilderness of Wirral; the detailed hunting scenes seem to be based on personal experience. So, too, with the landscape. Armour and costume are of the latest fashion. Even if the plot of *Gawain and the Green Knight* was French, the full-bodied narrative was English.

The three elements which were combined to make the framework of the poem were: the Beheading Game or Beheading Test; the Temptation; and the Exchange of Winnings. Taking up the first of these, let us recall that at Camelot on New Year's Day there appeared on a green horse a tall knight with green face and beard, and challenged any member of the Round Table to exchange with him a decapitating blow. Gawain accepted and cut off the challenger's head, but, as described above, the uncanny knight rode away. Amid the lamentations of the court Gawain set out ten months later to find the Green Chapel where he must submit his own neck to a return blow. He was entertained at the castle of a king, who sent him on New Year's Day with a guide to the spot. The Green Knight appeared, but, instead of chopping off Gawain's head, made two feints and then delivered so light a blow that he merely drew blood from the neck. He proclaimed Gawain the most faultless man who ever walked, and gave his own name as Sir Bercilak. There is the clearest of evidence that this series of events was derived from an old Irish tradition, for it combines features from two versions of the Beheading Game found side by side in the eighth-century saga of *Bricriu's Feast*.

In both versions an uncanny figure, bearing an axe, proposes the Beheading Game and allows Cuchulainn, one of the warriors of Ulster, to decapitate him. He returns the next day, however, and Cuchulainn in his turn submits his head to the axe. But the enchanter spares him and proclaims him the bravest of warriors. In the longer version the setting is the royal hall of Ulster. The enchanter, Curoi by name, is depicted as a gigantic churl (*bachlach*) in a dark-grey mantle; he taunts the assembled warriors with their cowardice; they lament when Cuchulainn seems to be doomed to death for his bravery. In the shorter version the setting of the test is beside a lake; on the way to it Cuchulainn and his rivals are entertained at a house and provided with a guide; the tester is a shapeshifter, and he delivers three strokes at Cuchulainn without harming him. Other details furnished by *Bricriu's Feast* make it apparent that the shapeshifter was a sky-god; as the dark-mantled wielder of a noisy axe, he personified the storm; as the light-bringer, who left his revolving home at night for a journey to the east and returned in the morning, he was manifestly the sun.

The second element is the Temptation. On three successive mornings, before his rendezvous with the Green Knight, Gawain was tempted by his beautiful hostess during her husband's absence on the chase; when he met the Green Knight at the end of a year it was at a water-crossing; the knight then admitted that he had connived at his wife's behaviour and praised Gawain's great fidelity. This element, the Temptation, also had its origin in Celtic myth: in the very first episode in the *Mabinogion*, as we saw in Chapter 2, a huntsman king, Arawn, connives that in his absence the hero, Pwyll, should lie nightly with his supremely beautiful wife; though sorely tempted, Pwyll turns his back on her out of fidelity to his host; Arawn, learning from his wife of Pwyll's behaviour, is deeply impressed with his resistance to carnal temptation and with his good faith. One could not ask for a clearer analogue and presumptive source for the Temptation than this eleventh-century Welsh tale.

But the tale is made up of far older elements. The motif of the Chaste Friend is found in an Egyptian narrative of about 1250 B.C. The anniversary combat derives from a myth of the struggle between Winter and Summer. Arawn is the mythical Wild Huntsman of European folklore, the personification of Winter's storms. His beautiful wife, though anonymous, is the multiform goddess Modron, who appears, as noted in Chapter 2, as one of a flock of ravens in the *Dream of Rhonabwy*. The

Gawain-poet was unaware, of course, of this remote and heathenish background, except for one touch: he, like three other medieval authors, recognized Morgan le Fay as a goddess.

The third element in the plot of *Gawain and the Green Knight* is the Exchange of Winnings. Gawain and his host, Sir Bercilak, agree to give each other at the end of each day whatever they have acquired. Scrupulously the huntsman surrendered to Gawain the spoils of the day's chase. Gawain, in turn, gave him the kisses which he had received from his wife. But, in violation of the bargain, he failed to pass on the magic girdle which might save his neck from the axe. Though the girdle is a traditional Arthurian feature of Celtic origin— Cuchulainn possessed a battle-belt from which lances and arrows would rebound—the Exchange of Winnings is a *fabliau* motif which crops up in the twelfth century. Its integration with the Celtic themes of the Beheading Test and the Temptation is so deft as to be little short of the miraculous. Without it they would fall apart; with it they form an extraordinarily coherent, though complicated, plot.

One ingenious theory, which has received favourable attention, would add to the artistic features of *Gawain and the Green Knight* a deliberate parallelism between Gawain's responses to the three seductive visits of his hostess, Sir Bercilak's wife, and the concurrent behaviour of the female deer, the boar, and the vixen hunted by his host. The theory is attractive, but if one reads the parallel passages expecting to find a striking correspondence, one will, I think, be disappointed. An author as clever as the *Gawain*-poet could have made the likeness much plainer if he had wished. But would an author as sensitive as he have wished to suggest a comparison between Gawain and beasts as timorous and defenceless as a hind, as savage as a boar, and as sly and thievish as a fox—and a female fox at that? Rather than see merit in an illusory parallelism, let us reserve our admiration for the main design of the poem, for the patterns of contrast so brilliantly executed, and the atmosphere of mystery and suspense which bespells the reader and lures him on.

Though the characters in *Gawain and the Green Knight* were bequeathed to the poet by tradition, nowhere does his creative genius display itself more conclusively than in their re-creation as full-bodied, psychologically realized beings. There is the Green Knight, derived partly from Curoi, partly from Arawn—two very dissimilar supernatural beings, yet both essentially friendly to the hero, though subjecting him to the severest tests. This inherited tradition of the two personalities furnished the poet with some of his best opportunities for un-canny effects and surprise. It offered him an opportunity to match the bargain to exchange blows with the bargain to exchange winnings, thus suggesting the identity of the Green Knight and Sir Bercilak. It left him, however, with the diffi-culty of explaining in realistic terms their motivation. The enmity of Morgan le Fay for Guenevere as the force which governed their conduct is rightly regarded by most critics as no solution, but a belated makeshift. Nevertheless, both the Green Knight and Sir Bercilak are entirely credible, vital actors in their respective roles. Indeed, the Green Knight, given his task to strike terror into the hearts of Arthur and his courtiers, does not miss a trick. On his green horse, he bursts into the hall with a great clatter. 'He rolls his red eyes, wags his great beard, boasts and taunts derisively, makes, after his decapitation, a tremendous exit.' But he gives, after all, the impression that he is 'a good fellow' and a great gentleman, for has he not taken the risk of decapitation and trusted Gawain to keep his part of the bargain?

In his second role as Gawain's hospitable host, there must be no trace of hostility. There is the same abounding vitality, however, manifested this time, both in the Christmas merry-making, and also in the strenuous activities of the chase. There is the same sporting spirit, and the same scrupulous observance of a bargain once made. It is not hard to believe, when his identity is revealed at last, that Sir Bercilak and the Green Knight are one—big-hearted, charged with energy, basically honourable and friendly.

The wife of the huntsman-host, as we have seen, was a

traditional temptress. In the *Mabinogion* her role was passive, but in the Arthurian romances it has become active, even aggressive. She turns up in the Swiss *Lanzelet* as the daughter of a forester and makes love to her father's guests by visiting them as they lie in bed, offering them a ring and making unambiguous proposals. Gawain's temptress uses the same opening move and later offers a ring, but she has a repertory of subtler tricks to win her game. Teasingly, she pins Gawain under the coverlet as a prisoner; she assures him that there is no danger of interruption; she flatters his vanity, especially referring to his reputation as an amorist. When he refuses to give her lessons in love, she charges him with rudeness, and, finally, she accuses him of having a mistress. Only after all these appeals to his sensual nature have failed does she tempt him with the girdle which will save his life, and so succeeds in making him betray his host. When we learn later that she was a tool of Morgan le Fay, without will of her own, all censure becomes nugatory, and we can only admire her brilliant performance as an actress in her role. And her light, gay touch contrasts with the sombre issues involved.

For the literary historian, looking back at Gawain's past, there can be few pursuits more fascinating than to observe the development of a noble and polished Christian knight from Cuchulainn, a barbaric demigod. Of course, the traits of bravery and fidelity to one's word were transmitted easily from the pagan to the medieval hero, and even Cuchulainn's solar nature offers the most plausible explanation of Gawain's uncanny habit of waxing in strength till noon, and then waning. From the Welsh Gwri of the Golden Hair Gawain inherited his name, a corruption of the epithet Gwallt-advwyn, meaning 'Bright Hair'. By the early twelfth century he had become Galvagin, Arthur's nephew and the nonpareil of his knights. In Chrétien's *Erec* he ranks first among the knights of the Round Table, and his courtesy presents a foil to the crudity and churlishness of Kay. Chaucer referred to his 'olde courtesye', and the Welsh took him back as Gwalchmai of the Golden Tongue.

But, for reasons not altogether clear, authors of the French prose romances began to degrade the character of Gawain, and Malory in parts of his work followed suit. The French poets made something of a Don Juan of him, but do not seem to think much the worse of him for that. In England his early reputation for valour and virtue seems to have gone un-challenged till Malory, but it was a confused tradition which the *Gawain*-poet had to handle. That he made out of this con-fusion a character so consistent, so living, and so likeable is the surest proof of his genius, even though the main features were probably outlined in his French source. The fundamental warrior's qualities of bravery and loyalty are softened, though not weakened, by the courtier's virtues of modesty and gracious speech, enriched by humour and cleverness, and sublimated by Christian piety and a keen sense of honour. But Gawain is not a Galahad, invulnerable to temptation; he feels the strong stirrings of lust and the terror of death.

In accepting the challenge of the Green Knight, from which all the other knights shrank, he does only what is expected of any hero of medieval romance. What is noteworthy is his manner of accepting it: his apology to the Queen for leaving his place beside her; his profession of unworthiness for the task, except on the ground of his relation to the King; his request to be pardoned if he has spoken amiss. This is Gawain, the model of manners, and yet so deftly rendered that one does not doubt his sincerity. His courage and his sense of honour are tested when he sets out alone for his perilous rendezvous at the Green Chapel; and the poet leaves no doubt of the hardships of the journey. Though facing imminent death, Gawain is the perfect guest at Sir Bercilak's castle, playing up to the frolicsome mood of his host and hostess.

Most natural and yet most subtly treated are his reactions to the seductive manœuvres of the lady. At first, taken by sur-prise, he pretends to be asleep. When she makes a frank offer of love, he does not bluntly reject it; he declares himself honoured to be 'her knight'—a platonic relationship—and calls on Christ to reward her for this favour. When she begs him, as an expert amorist, to give her some lessons, he modestly and flatteringly defers to her superior knowledge. Thus he matches wits with her, and has a riposte for every thrust. Despite his awkward situation, Gawain never becomes ridiculous, like Fielding's Joseph Andrews, solicited by Lady Booby. At the third visit he nearly succumbs to the physical charms of his temptress, but he cannot bring himself to betray his host. It is only when he is enticed by the offer of the magic girdle that he yields to fear what he would not yield to lust, and by concealing the gift from his host breaks his word.

Yet, impelled by his sense of honour, hoping that the girdle will afford him protection, Gawain rides to the Green Chapel. The gloomy, savage landscape renews his fears. But, true to his compact, when the Green Knight appears out of a hole in the hillside above him, vaults over a brook with the aid of an axe, and demands the fulfilment of the bargain, Gawain bares his neck. He cannot help flinching as the huge blade descends in a feint. He steadies himself, but when, a second time, the blow proves to be a feint, he angrily demands an end to the fooling, and awaits his doom. As soon as he realizes that the third blow has caused only a flesh wound, he bounds away, draws his sword, and defies the monster to attempt another stroke. Suddenly the monster changes his tune, discloses the plot, puts the blame on Morgan, and invites Gawain back to the castle to enjoy the rest of the New Year festivities. Though bewildered and humiliated, Gawain still follows the dictates of courtesy to the extent of sending his greetings to his late hostess, but very naturally declines the invitation and ventilates his feelings in a tirade against the female sex. He finds his way back to Arthur's court, repentant, wearing the green girdle as a sign of shame. But the knights and ladies refuse to recognize it as such and adopt it as the badge of honour.

Seldom in literature has an ideal type been endowed with such a many-faceted, credible, warm humanity. Seldom have chivalric idealism, Christian ethics, and vivid realism been so happily blended. Somewhat similar is Wolfram's accomplish-

THE ALLITERATIVE ENGLISH ROMANCES 163

ment in the portrayal of the mature Parzival. Both heroes present a contrast to Lancelot, Guenevere's slave, untrue to his king and his God; both, on the other hand, contrast with Galahad, ascetic, unworldly, sinless, immune to temptation. Both fall short of perfection, Gawain by breaking his word, Parzival by his lack of compassion; both are deeply repentant; both are welcomed back with love and admiration to the fellowship of the Round Table. Indeed, both come to typify at the end a happy harmonization of the secular ideal of honour with obedience to the dictates of religion.

What, then, is the dominant purpose, the 'sen' of *Gawain and the Green Knight*? Many are the answers offered by modern criticism. One critic finds it a study in colour symbolism, a struggle between the green (signifying Nature and the primitive instincts of Man) and gold (signifying the comforts and codes of civilization). That the poet intentionally contrasted the warm gay interiors of Camelot and Sir Bercilak's castle with the bleak wintry world outside, few would question, but it seems doubtful whether anyone but the author of the article would find this opposition the key to the poem, especially since the final choice of the green baldric by the knights and ladies of the Round Table would have to be interpreted as a preference for primitive instincts over civilization. Surely a curious moral for the author of *Patience* and *Purity*.

Another critic with a numerous clientele, recognizing the pagan background of the poem, opines that the Beheading Test mirrors a rite which survived into the fourteenth century and might have been observed by the poet himself. Somewhat inconsistently the critic would identify the Green Knight with the Green Man, who takes part in May Day celebrations in England today, completely encased in a framework of leaves, a sort of walking bush. But there is nothing but the adjective 'green' to connect the two figures. No entirely convincing explanation of the colour has been proposed. Both Curoi and Arawn, prototypes of the Green Knight in his dual aspects, were clad in grey. It should be obvious, however, that whatever mythological significance is to be discovered in the poem must be inferred from *Bricriu's Feast* and *Pwyll*, and not from English May Day festivals, no matter how ancient they may be. That the author reproduced in his poem heathenish rites, practised in the forests of the north, is not even a plausible guess.

Even more incredible is the theory that the devoutly Christian poet's main intention was to proclaim the primacy of amoral, generic forces over Christian and chivalric values. This is as absurd as the medieval attempt to interpret Ovid's *Metamorphoses*, full of amoral, generic forces, as a collection of pious parables.

Let me recall the witty remark of Professor C. S. Lewis:

> Some published fantasies of my own have had foisted on them (often by the kindliest critics) so many admirable allegorical meanings that I never dreamed of as to throw me into doubt whether it is possible for the wit of man to devise anything in which the wit of some other man cannot find, and plausibly find, an allegory.

If, then, these arbitrary efforts to find a hidden meaning may be dismissed, the question remains whether the poet intended any arcane symbolisms or allegories which lie deep beneath the surface. (Remember that we are in the fourteenth and not the twentieth century.) There is a passage which has an obvious bearing on the question. Gawain's shield bore the device of a pentangle, a sort of five-pointed star, and its significance the author explains in detail. Gawain, as a paragon of Christian knighthood, was faultless in his five senses, was skilled in the use of his five fingers, trusting in the five wounds of Christ, strengthened by the thought of the five joys of Mary, and endowed with the five virtues of generosity, love, chastity, courtesy, and, greatest of all, pity. As a didactic writer—and surely the author of *Patience*, *Purity*, and the *Pearl* was one—the *Gawain*-poet took pains to ensure that any symbolic or other esoteric meaning which he intended was made clear. It is safe to infer that when such meanings were not expounded in the text, they did not exist. (Incidentally, the exaltation of pity as the highest of the five virtues provides additional evidence of a spiritual kinship between the *Gawain*-poet and Wolfram von Eschenbach, who made the crucial test of Parzival a trial of compassion for the agonies of Anfortas; a kinship, too, with Chaucer, whose favourite line, four times repeated, was: 'For pitee renneth soon in gentil herte'; that is: 'For pity flows at once in noble heart'.)

To find the 'sen', the main point which our author intended, should not require much detective work, much digging below the surface. We need only to read the text, particularly the last two stanzas which tell how the hero returned wearing the green girdle as a token of shame, and how it was adopted by the court as a badge of honour. The most perceptive restatement of what was surely the poet's intention is that of Laura Hibbard Loomis:

> In this Gawain, the blithe young embodiment of chivalry at its best, goodness is made manifest and radiant, but not, as in Galahad of the Grail romances, a supernatural virtue touched by a mysterious divinity. The 'fine issue' of his story is not that he fell into vulgar sin, but that he failed to keep goodness perfect. Moral earnestness could hardly go further. Gawain's confession of his fault in breaking his word to save his life reveals a deep sense of Man's responsibility for his every act, no matter how deadly the betraying circumstance. . . . Wholeheartedly Gawain recognizes this rigorous truth and contrition overwhelms him. Unlike other Arthurian heroes, he returns to Arthur's court, not in conventional glory, but in self-confessed shame. Yet, as noted above, that shame gave him new grace, and the Round Table achieved a new nobility by its act of compassionate fellowship.

SIR THOMAS MALORY

In 1469 or 1470 an aged knight, writing in prison, as King James I of Scotland had done before and as John Bunyan was to do long after, penned these final words:

> I pray you all, gentlemen and gentlewomen, that readeth this book of Arthur and his knights from the beginning to the ending, pray for me while I am on live that God send me good deliverance; and when I am dead, I pray you all pray for my soul.

He signed his name, Sir Thomas Malory, 'as Jesu help him for His great might, as he is the servant of Jesu both day and night'. Some fifteen years later, in 1485, the enterprising William Caxton, the first English printer, obtained a manuscript of Malory's work, divided it somewhat arbitrarily into twenty-one books, divided these in turn into chapters, and by mistake and in disregard of French grammar gave the whole work the title *Le Morte d'Arthur*, by which it is still generally known. Only one complete copy of this first edition printed at Westminster survives and is now in the Morgan Library, New York. In 1934 a unique manuscript was discovered at Winchester College, which, though it is by no means an accurate transcript of Malory's autograph, shows us nevertheless the state in which he left his work and confirms the opinion that he composed it in prison.

Before considering the author and his work, let us give our attention briefly to his editor and publisher. Caxton, born in Kent, was sent at the age of nineteen as an apprentice to the prosperous cloth-weaving centre of Bruges, and in 1463 had become Governor of the English Nation of Merchant Adventurers in the Low Countries. In 1469, at the age of forty-seven, he began translating a French romance of Troy; in the next two years he investigated the process of printing from movable type at Cologne; and in 1475 brought out at Bruges his translation, the first English book to be printed. The next year he set up his press at Westminster and, until his death in 1491, continued to publish a wide variety of books—pious, practical, historical, satirical, entertaining. These included twenty-four translated by himself and some of the works of Chaucer, Gower, and Lydgate. Though no great writer himself, he did much to make literature available to the increasingly literate middle class and the aristocracy. Among his patrons he numbered three kings as well as great earls and merchants.

In his preface Caxton gave an illuminating account of the circumstances which led to the publication of Malory's book. Many gentlemen had reproached him for his failure to print the noble history of the Saint Greal and of the most renowned Christian king, Arthur, who ought to be remembered 'among us Englishmen before all other Christian kings'. Was it not known throughout the world that Arthur was one of the nine greatest warriors of history? (This was a reference to the so-called Nine Worthies frequently represented in tapestry, sculpture, and mural painting of the late Middle Ages.) Caxton at first excused himself on the ground that divers men held that all books made about Arthur were but feigned and fables, but he was finally convinced by such tangible evidences as the tomb of Arthur at Glastonbury (actually the result of a 'plant' perpetrated in 1191), the Round Table, which is still to be seen at Winchester, Gawain's skull and Cradok's mantle at Dover Castle, which have long since disappeared. So Caxton procured the text, which Malory 'reduced into English' from certain French books, edited it, and printed it. He assured his readers that they would find in it 'noble chivalry, courtesy, humanity, friendliness, hardiness, love, friendship, cowardice, murder, hate, virtue, and sin. Do after the good and leave the evil, and it shall bring you to good fame and renown.' As to believing that all was true, however, the canny Kentishman left it to the reader's choice.

Who was the author of the *Morte d'Arthur*, or, as he called it, the *Book of King Arthur and His Noble Knights*? His forebears held estates in Warwickshire and Leicestershire, and on the death of his father in 1434 he came into the property. Two years later, it seems, he served at the siege of Calais under the command of the Earl of Warwick, Richard Beauchamp, whose splendid bronze image still lies in the church of St Mary's, Warwick, on a marble tomb. This Richard had a spectacular career in the French war, including jousts in different arms on three successive days; visited Jerusalem, where, as the descendant of the legendary Guy of Warwick, he was welcomed even by the Turks; and so impressed the Emperor at the Council of Constance by his gracious behaviour that the Emperor declared that if all courtesy were lost, yet it might be found again in him. We next hear of Sir Thomas Malory as sitting in Parliament in 1445. His name appears in a list of knights who under another Earl of Warwick marched into Northumberland against the Lancastrians in 1462. Unaccountably, six years later he was excluded from a royal pardon granted to the Lancastrians. He died in 1471, and his grave in the Franciscan church near Newgate prison bore the inscription 'valens miles'.

These facts would lead one to surmise that the Warwickshire knight, like his commander at Calais, was a pattern of chivalry. But investigators have discovered, mainly in the Public Record Office, a considerable number of documents alleging that this very same Sir Thomas, between 1450 and 1460, committed a wide variety of crimes, such as an attempt to murder the Duke of Buckingham, breaking into the abbey of Combe two days in succession, twice raping the same woman, stealing cattle, and a mere non-payment of debt. Twice he escaped from prison, once by swimming a moat, once together with a group armed with swords, daggers, and halberds. But most of that decade he seems to have spent behind bars, and evidently, as we have seen, he was in his last years a prisoner too dangerous for the Yorkists to let loose.

It is premature to form an opinion as to Malory's guilt. Only when someone familiar with the political and social history of England during the Wars of the Roses, thoroughly acquainted with the operation of the law and its devious ways, interprets the documents will there be a real basis for judgment. Until then let us note that Malory was never convicted, only indicted, and indictments seem to have been used by the unscrupulous as a means of putting innocent but troublesome people out of the way. For example, Sir John Fastolf, Malory's contemporary, ordered one of his agents to indict, whatever the cost, all those jurors who opposed his interests. Even if there was some basis in fact for the charges against Malory, even if he resorted to violence on more than one occasion, the turbulent condition of England may have justified him. He himself pleaded not guilty to the gravest accusations, and the only offence he acknowledged was failure to pay a debt. After all, is it likely that a scoundrel composed the oath taken by the knights of the Round Table: 'never to do outrage nor murder, and always to flee treason, and to give mercy to him that asketh mercy . . . and always to do ladies, damsels, and gentlewomen and widows succour, strengthen them in their rights, and never to enforce them; . . . also that no man take no battles in a wrongful quarrel for no love ne for no world's goods'? To accept as proved the charges brought against Malory is to believe that he was both a hardened criminal and a hypocrite.

His book is a compilation from at least nine principal sources, and since several of them were very bulky and expensive it is unlikely that they were his own property. It has been plausibly suggested that the prisoner in Newgate availed himself of the large library which Whittington, the famous mayor of London, had established in the Grey Friars' precincts close by; but, in a period when books were so precious that they had to be chained, they would hardly be released to the inmate of a gaol.

Using the division into books adopted by Caxton, let us see what the various sources were. The first four books are a condensed and rearranged translation of the French prose romance known as the *Huth Merlin* or the *Suite du Merlin*, written between 1230 and 1240. Book V is an abridgment of the *Alliterative Morte Arthur*. Book VI is a translation of three separate extracts from the *Vulgate Lancelot*. Book VII followed a lost Anglo-Norman romance of Gareth. The next five books form an abridged and incomplete rendering of the tedious *Prose Tristan*, dated about 1230. They lead up to the Vulgate version of the quest of the Grail, which forms the subject of Books XIII to XVII. A prosaic and very English version of the abduction and rescue of Guenevere makes up Book XIX and was based on a lost source. The remaining Books, XVIII, XX, and XXI, contain a drastic and masterly rehandling of the last days of the Round Table, blending the account in the *Vulgate Mort Artu* with that in the English poem, the *Stanzaic Morte Arthur*.

Malory was limited, of course, in his choice of material by the number of manuscripts available to him. One could have wished that he had followed Thomas or Béroul in treating the loves of Tristan and Isolt, but the French verse romances had long been out of fashion, and doubtless the tedious and debased *Prose Tristan* was the only version he knew. The adulterous passion of Lancelot for Guenevere is one of the major themes of Malory's work, but it is suddenly thrust upon our attention in Book V as a *fait accompli*. Lacking are the charming scenes which deal with the nascent love of the bashful youth and the amorous Queen. The blame for this omission lies not with Malory but with the incomplete state of the *Prose Lancelot* which he used. On the other hand, many of the large cuts which he made in his sources were dictated by common sense. From the *Suite du Merlin* he dropped the early history of the mage and Uther's wars with the Saxons and began with the events immediately preceding the conception of Arthur. On the whole, we may say that from the literature that was available to him Malory made his selection with sound judgment;

and, as we shall presently see, he displayed in his treatment of that material a steadily progressive artistry.

The variety of his sources contributed both to the defects and the virtues of his compilation. Inconsistencies, of course, abound, but many of the chronological difficulties vanish when one realizes that the author sometimes deliberately retrogressed, and so a character slain in one book may be resuscitated in the next. Other discrepancies are too inconsequential to be noticed, or, if noticed, may well be excused because of the conglomerate nature of the work.

Far more serious flaws, arising from the diversity of sources, are the conflicting concepts of three major characters—Kay, Gawain, and Arthur himself. When Sir Kay first appears on the scene he is the deceitful lad who falsely claims the kingship of England, but presently he is Arthur's trusted seneschal, performing great feats of arms in a tourney, only to turn up in Book VII as a churlish mocker, easily unhorsed by young Sir Gareth. In Book IV Gawain is depicted as a treacherous bounder; in Book VII he is described as 'vengeable' and murderous; but in the last book Arthur mourns him as 'the man in the world that I loved most', and sees him in a vision surrounded by ladies whom God had permitted to appear with him because he had done battle for their rights. As for Arthur, 'the most renowned Christian King', before the end of Book I he has begotten two bastards and has attempted to destroy all the lords' sons born on May Day—an act which reminds one all too vividly of the slaughter of the innocents by King Herod.

These gross inconsistencies in characterization have a bearing on the much debated question of the unity of Malory's work. Did he conceive of it as a loose gathering together of eight or more independent, self-contained tales, united solely by their attachment to the court of King Arthur? Or did he make an effort to tie them together to form a coherent whole?

There is no evidence as to the author's original conception of his task when he first put quill-pen to parchment. But if at the time his future seemed as uncertain as his past had been, it is very unlikely that he contemplated any grandiose project. Several of the early tales—the Balin, the war with Lucius, the Gareth—not only were derived from different sources, but can still be read as separate units. The *explicits* which conclude these tales were not put there for nothing. It seems probable that some of them were undertaken without thought of any larger, comprehensive design, and that, even when he had stitched them together, Malory still regarded them as distinct enterprises.

On the other hand, long before he completed his task, he surely recognized that the units could be worked into a larger, somewhat coherent whole, and, either in the course of composition or in revising, he took measures to achieve this coherence. He introduced sentences or paragraphs of transition to bridge the gaps between the tales. He made clear the chronological relationships between them. He modified his sources to make of Lancelot a more consistently noble character; throughout the series of tales, Lancelot exhibits boundless courage, good sportsmanship, friendliness, and magnanimity. His passion for the Queen is ennobled by his constancy and patience.

Another proof that the *Book of Arthur and His Noble Knights* was regarded by its author as more than a haphazard collocation of separate units is provided by his references forward and backward. At the end of Book I we find two such anticipations: a reference to Mordred's coming to Arthur's court, 'as it rehearseth afterward and toward the end of the *Morte Arthur*'; a mention of the gathering of King Rience's host, 'as it rehearseth in the Book of Balin le Savage that followeth next after'. The Book of Balin, in turn, concludes with the announcement that Galahad would achieve the adventure of the sword in the floating stone, 'as it is rehearsed in the Book of the Sangreal'; and when Galahad has achieved the adventure, he makes a speech (not found in the French source) referring to the sword as having belonged once to the good knight Balin le Savage. Thus in several ways Malory endeavoured to give coherence and harmony to his compilation. And he wrote in the final colophon: 'Here is the end of the *whole book* of King Arthur and his noble knights.'

The controversy over the unity of Malory's works resembles a debate on the question: Are the United States of America separate or united? The answer is that they are both separate and united. Malory by his *explicits* and in other ways recognized the separateness of the tales, but he also fitted them together into one 'whole book'.

In spite of his efforts to achieve coherence and consistency, he failed—and could not help failing—to attain a complete organic unity. Besides the discrepancies and contradictions already cited, there is a wide variety of tone. What a gap in style, ideology, and feeling between the tale of Arthur's war with the Emperor Lucius and the tale of the Sangreal. The one borrows its pompous style from the Anglo-Saxon tradition, glorifies conquest and cruelty, and makes a fine art of boasting and insult; the other is written in an austere, plain style, reprobates manslaughter, and breathes the spirit of its Cistercian model.

This lack of harmony detracts, of course, from Malory's masterpiece as a work of art, but for the historical student of literature the variety of styles, moods, and standards has its compensations. Like the Bible, the *Book of King Arthur and His Noble Knights* is an assemblage of materials from different peoples and epochs, and looks at life from shifting points of view. There is a fascination in watching the kaleidoscopic changes in colour and dominant pattern as one passes from tale to tale. The first, comprising Books I to IV, is pervaded and controlled by the heathenish magic of Merlin; the account of the Roman war is charged with the chauvinistic passion roused by the Hundred Years' War; the doctrine of divine grace furnishes the *leit-motif* of the quest of the Grail; a series of fatalistic accidents combines with the faults of the chief characters to bring about the downfall of the Round Table. To the serious student of medieval culture this variety can be of absorbing interest, and to the casual reader it affords relief from monotony. When battles and tournaments pall and magic and marvels lose their charm, there are heavenly visions and powerful scenes of psychological conflict and grim tragedy.

Malory was an uneven writer. Educated in the school of hard knocks rather than in the schools of Oxford or Cambridge —to be sure, one could be knocked about there, if one may judge by the records of town-and-gown riots—he was as careless of grammar and syntax as any knight of the Round Table. When Arthur bade Bedivere cast Excalibur into the lake, Bedivere replied: 'My lord, your commandment shall be done, and lightly bring you word again.' The much admired lament of Sir Ector for his brother Lancelot, which is Malory's expansion of two lines in the *Stanzaic Morte Arthur* ('The best knight his life has lorn That ever in stour bestrode a steed'), would not have satisfied a rhetorician.

> 'Ah Lancelot, thou were head of all Christian knights! And now I dare say, thou Sir Lancelot, there thou liest, thou were never matched of earthly knight's hand. And thou were the courteoust knight that ever bare shield! And thou were the truest friend to thy lover that ever bestrode horse, and thou were the truest lover of a sinful man that ever loved woman, and thou were the kindest man that ever struck with sword! And thou were the goodliest person that ever came among press of knights, and thou was the meekest man and the gentlest that ever ate in hall among ladies, and thou were the sternest knight to thy mortal foe that ever put spear in the rest!'

What could be more absurd than to praise Lancelot for being the kindest man who ever struck with sword, for a sword stroke is anything but an act of kindness. But, by a sort of paradox, it is the very crudeness of such discourse which makes it ring true. Sir Bedivere and Sir Ector were not the men to correct their sentences before they spoke them, and grief does not obey the laws of logic.

Though often the faults of Malory's style may be reckoned as merits, this is not always so. Take the familiar prelude to his account of the abduction of Guenevere by Mellyagraunce.

Like as trees and herbs burgeon and flourish in May, in like wise every lusty heart that is any manner of lover springeth, burgeoneth, buddeth, and flourisheth in lusty deeds. For it giveth unto all lovers courage, that lusty month of May, in something to constrain him to some manner of thing more than in any other month, for divers causes; for then all herbs and trees renew a man and woman, and in like wise lovers call to their mind old gentleness and old service, and many kind deeds that was forgotten by negligence. For, like as winter rasure doth alway raze and deface green summer, so fareth it by unstable love in man and woman, for in many persons there is no stability; for we may see all day, for a little blast of winter's rasure, anon we shall deface and lay apart true love, for little or naught, that cost much thing. This is no wisdom nor no stability, but it is feebleness of nature and great disworship, whosoever useth this.

After a dozen more sentences, the passage concludes:

Therefore, all ye that be lovers, call unto your remembrance the month of May, like as did Queen Guenevere, for whom I make here a little mention that while she lived, she was a true lover, and therefore she had a good end.

This passage has been described as one of the quaintest and most delightfully cadenced bits of medieval prose; and quaint and cadenced it may well be. But it is also clumsy and fumbling, and in spite of the number of conjunctive 'therefores' and 'fors' the thought meanders. It would be charitable to suppose that when Sir Thomas indited his little dithyramb in praise of May and constancy in love he had been imbibing freely of a certain product of Bordeaux.

Yet it was this same author who not only integrated the disparate elements of his book with what, considering the circumstances, was a remarkable success, but also showed great cleverness in 'reducing' his French texts, and achieved in his last books a style unpretentious, dignified, taut, poignant, 'blending', as has been said, 'the majesty of epic eloquence with the freshness of living speech'.

He shows this talent already in Caxton's Book II, the Book of Balin. Its source is the so-called *Suite du Merlin*, which provided a series of episodes linking the prose version of Robert's *Merlin* to the *Quest of the Holy Grail* and the *Mort Artu*. Into this fabric the French author wove the story of Balin, which may well have existed once as a separate *conte*. Malory, recognizing its independence and its unity, disengaged it partly from its context and made it 'The Book of Balin'. He reduced it to one-fourth and made it by due subordination and omission the powerful narrative which inspired Tennyson and Swinburne to re-tell it in their own ways. Perhaps Malory felt a certain kinship to the unhappy hero; without question he sharply emphasized the concept of Balin as a man bold, impetuous, well-meaning, but doomed, like the Greek Orestes, to disaster. The words 'dole' and 'dolorous' recur throughout the story like the tolling of a bell.

Balin first appears at Arthur's court as a poor knight from Northumberland, who has been imprisoned for killing one of the King's relatives. To a damsel who put a slight on him because of his shabby garb, he replied proudly: 'Ah, fair damsel, worthiness and good tatches and good deeds are not only in arrayment, but manhood and worship is hid within man's person.' This speech is significantly altered from the French, where Balin boasts, not of his character but of his former wealth. When the damsel warns him that he will kill with a certain sword the man he most loves in the world, he bluntly replies: 'I shall take the adventure that God will ordain me, but the sword ye shall not have at this time, by the faith of my body.' Later, when Merlin tells him that, because he had caused, though blamelessly, the death of a knight and his lady, he was destined to wound the man of most worship then living, and bring woe to three kingdoms, Balin breaks out: 'If I wist it were sooth that ye say, I should do such a perilous deed as that, I would slay myself to make thee a liar!' Later the prophecy is fulfilled. The lord of the Grail castle, here called King Pellam, attacks Balin, and Balin in self-defence smites the King with the spear which pierced the side of the crucified Christ. The King falls in a swoon, the castle crashes about him, and as Balin rides away at last the few people who survive cry out: 'O Balin, thou hast caused great damage in these countries; for the dolorous stroke thou gavest unto King Pellam three countries are destroyed, and doubt not that the vengeance shall fall on thee at the last.'

The sense of fatality and helplessness deepens. Balin came by a cross, 'and thereon were letters of gold written, that said: "It is not for no knight alone to ride toward this castle." Then saw he an old hoar gentleman coming toward him, that said: "Balin le Savage, thou passest thy bounds to come this way; therefore turn again and it will avail thee." And he vanished away anon; and so he heard an horn blow as it had been the death of a beast. "That blast," said Balin, "is blown for me, for I am the prize"—that is, the captive beast—"and yet am I not dead." ' But death soon follows. By unhappy chance he exchanges his shield for a bigger one. Thus, unrecognized, he meets his brother in a desperate combat, and each mortally wounds the other. The issue of one womb, the two are buried in one grave.

In the *Suite du Merlin* this story of a great-hearted victim of fate is well told, but the style is leisurely and at times verbose. Malory by omission of irrelevant detail, by compression, and by altering sometimes the sense or the phrasing of Balin's utterances, magnifies the impact of the tale. And he emphasizes the courage of his hero. When Merlin in an early meeting with the brothers warns them: 'Look ye do knightly, for ye shall have great need,' Balin replies: 'As for that, dread you not; we will do what we may.' And at the last, knowing that his time is short, he exclaims: 'Me repenteth that ever I came within this country, but I may not turn now again for shame. . . . Be it life or death, I will take the adventure that shall come to me.'

Book VII, the story of Gareth of Orkney, Gawain's brother, is another of Malory's successes, but in a very different vein. We cannot compare it with its source, for that is lost. But it must have been written by an Anglo-Norman in French, for only an Anglo-Norman would have spelled Garet with a *th*, and have imagined that Beaumayns, Gareth's nickname, was good French for 'Fair-Hands'. Ultimately, the story of a damsel who comes to court to seek a champion for her besieged mistress was derived from the ninth-century Irish saga, the *Wasting Sickness of Cuchulainn*; in fact, the French version of the story is attached to a knight named Guinglain. Since we cannot compare Malory's version with its Anglo-Norman source, we are unable to determine how faithfully he followed it; it is clear, however, that he could enter into the spirit of light comedy as into the mood of grim tragedy.

Like Balin, Gareth had courage, but, unlike him, he acted with forethought, patience, and restraint. Moreover, Fortune was not his foe but his friend. When the damsel Lynet appeared at Arthur's court to ask succour for her sister, Dame Lyones, Gareth, who had been serving at his own request as a scullion, claimed the dangerous assignment, and Arthur, bound by his promise, granted it. A piquant situation developed as the recent kitchen-boy rode after Lynet, who had departed in disgust. She called out: 'What dost thou here? Thou stinkest all of the kitchen; thy clothes be bawdy of grease and tallow. . . . What art thou but a lusk and a turner of broaches and a ladle-washer?' The well-mannered Gareth replied: 'Damsel, say to me what ye will, I will not go from you whatsoever ye say, for I have undertaken to King Arthur for to achieve your adventure, and so shall I finish it to the end, either I shall die therefor.' Furious at his calm persistence, Lynet threatened him with such a foe as 'thou wouldest not for all the broth that ever thou suppest once look him in the face'. 'As for that,' said Beaumayns, 'I shall essay.' Throughout the whole Book of Gareth, Malory maintains the same vivacity and naturalness of dialogue.

It seems natural, too, that Gareth should fall in love not

with the vinegar-tongued Lynet, but with her passionate sister
Dame Lyones, and natural, too, that after he has proved his
prowess and devotion to the full, there should ensue the
following colloquy:

> The King asked his nephew, Sir Gareth, whether he
> would have that lady as paramour, or to have her to his
> wife. 'My lord, wit you well that I love her above all ladies
> living.' 'Now, fair lady,' said King Arthur, 'what say ye?'
> 'Most noble king,' said Dame Lyones, 'wit you well that
> my lord, Sir Gareth, is to me more liefer to have and wield
> as my husband than any king or prince that is christened;
> and if I may not have him, I promise you I will never have
> none. For, my lord Arthur, wit ye well he is my first love,
> and he shall be the last; and if ye will suffer him to have
> his will and free choice, I dare say he will have me.' 'That
> is truth,' said Sir Gareth; 'an I have not you and wield not
> you as my wife, there shall never lady nor gentlewoman
> rejoice me.' 'What, nephew,' said the King, 'is the wind
> in that door? For wit ye well I would not for the stint of
> my crown to be causer to withdraw your hearts; and wit
> ye well ye cannot love so well but I shall rather increase
> it than discrease it.'

A condensed version of the long-winded *Prose Tristan*
occupies a third of Malory's book. His patience seems to have
given out at last, and he dropped the subject without relating
how, finally, King Mark killed Tristan with a trenchant
glaive as he was harping before Queen Isolt—though there is
casual mention of this ending later. For the story of the Grail
Malory followed faithfully the French *Quest*, suppressing, however, some banal homilies by the ubiquitous hermits and
presenting the sinner, Lancelot, in a more favourable light
than the Cistercian author had done. He proved himself able
to match the sublimity of the great scenes, as in the description,
already mentioned in Chapter 7, of the appearance of the
Grail to the knights of the Round Table:

Then anon they heard cracking and crying of thunder that them thought the palace should all to-drive. In the midst of this blast entered a sunbeam more clearer by seven times than ever they saw day, and all they were alighted of the grace of the Holy Ghost. Then began every knight to behold other, and either saw other by their seeming fairer than ever they saw afore. Not for then there was no knight might speak one word a great while, and so they looked every man on other as they had been dumb. Then there entered into the hall the Holy Grail, covered with white samite, but there was none might see it, nor who bare it. And there was all the hall fulfilled with good odours, and every knight had such meats and drinks as he best loved in this world.

If the Grail books are the least original of Malory's renderings from the French, the last books dealing with the exposure of the liaison between Lancelot and Guenevere, the war between Lancelot and the King, the treachery of Modred, the passing of Arthur, and the parting of Lancelot and the Queen are the freest and the greatest. Wisely Malory preserved the main outline of events as narrated in the *Vulgate Mort Artu*, and took over from that source the clear and realistic portrayals of the main characters in the tragedy: Arthur, pitifully torn between the obligation to punish his guilty queen and the realization that to do so would mean death to those he loved and ruin to his kingdom; Gawain, staunchly loyal to Arthur, devoted likewise to Lancelot, until unwittingly Lancelot kills Gaheris and Gareth, and becomes his implacable foe; Lancelot, swayed at first by the duty to save his paramour from the flames, then magnanimously yielding to the Pope's pressure and restoring her to Arthur, making every effort to avoid war with his liege lord and friend, twice sparing Gawain's life in mortal combat; Guenevere, the pitiful victim of clashing forces, yet clever and strong enough to save herself from Modred, strong enough, too, in resolution to forbid her lover to see her again after she had taken the vows.

But though the majestic finale of the *Book of King Arthur and His Noble Knights* owes the firmness of its texture and the fine consistency of its characterization to the *Mort Artu*, Malory tells a more vivid and affecting story. The French classic is too prolix and at times too rhetorical. Malory not only omits and abridges, but completely recasts, and inserts new matter; and every change or addition is for the better. There is nothing in the French quite so poignant as this dialogue which precedes the first combat between Lancelot and Gawain.

> Lancelot loudly speaks to Arthur: 'My lord Arthur and noble king that made me knight, wit you well I am right heavy for your sake, that ye thus sue upon me; and always I forbare you, for, an I would have been vengeable, I might have met you in the midst of the field and there to have made your boldest knights full tame. And now I have forborne half a year and suffered you and Sir Gawain to do what ye would do; and now may I endure it no longer, for now must I needs defend myself, insomuch Sir Gawain hath appealed me of treason; the which is greatly against my will that ever I should fight against any of your blood, but now I may not forsake it, I am driven thereto as a beast till a bay.'

Note the simile of the stag or boar at bay. Gawain shouts back: 'An thou durst do battle, leave thy babbling and come off, and let us ease our hearts!' Note the insulting 'thou' and 'thy'.

Paradoxically speaking, it is one consequence of Malory's independence that in departing from the *Mort Artu* he comes to lean more and more on the *Stanzaic Morte Arthur*, a poem of the late fourteenth century, patently the attempt of an English minstrel to versify what he remembered of the French romance. It is another paradox that from this mediocre poem, full of stereotyped phrases, Malory derived some of his most memorable passages. The whole scene between the wounded

Arthur and Bedivere, though there is a corresponding scene in the French, is almost a paraphrase of the English poem.

> 'What saw thou there?' then said the king;
> 'Tell me now if thou can.'
> 'Certes, sir,' he said, 'no thing
> But waters deep and wawes wan.'

Malory, it will be remembered, has: 'What saw thou there?' said the King. 'Sir,' he said, 'I saw nothing but the waters wap and waves wan.' Here with a characteristic scorn of grammar, and with a touch of genius, he substituted the verb *wap* meaning 'lap' for the adjective *deep*, and thereby forced the adjective *wan*, meaning 'dark', to become a verb also. And though the result leaves the purist wondering how waves can wan, it also perfectly conveys the onomatopoetic effect of lapping waters.

The *Morte Arthur* thus gives the final words between Arthur and Bedivere:

> The knight cast a rueful roun,   (uttered a pitiful moan)
> Where he stood, sore and unsound,   (weak)
> And said: 'Lord, whither are ye bound?
> Alas, whither will ye from me found?'   (go)
> The king spake with a sorry sound:
> 'I will wend a little stound   (time)
> Into the Vale of Aveloun,
> Awhile to heal me of my wound.'

This is Malory's version:

> Then Sir Bedivere cried and said: 'Ah my lord Arthur, what shall become of me, now ye go from me and leave me here alone among mine enemies?' 'Comfort thyself,' said the King, 'and do as well as thou mayst, for in me is no trust for to trust in. For I must into the vale of Avilion to

heal me of my grievous wound. And if thou hear nevermore of me, pray for my soul!'

Again Malory displayed his genius for selection when he described a final meeting between Lancelot and Guenevere after she had taken the veil—a scene not found in the standard text of the *Mort Artu*, but elaborated from a variant French text by the poet of the *Stanzaic Morte Arthur*. The Queen swoons at sight of her former lover, and, on recovering, addresses the abbess:

'Abbess, to you I knowledge here
That through this ilka man and me—   (same)
For we together have loved us dear—
All this sorrowful war hath be;
My lord is slain, that had no peer,
And many a doughty knight and free;   (generous)
Therefore for sorrow I died near   (nearly)
As soon as I ever gan him see. . . .

'Yset I am in such a place,   (set)
My soul's heal I will abide,
Till God send me some grace,
Through mercy of His woundes wide;
That I may do so in this place
My sins to amend this ilka tide,
After to have a sight of His face
At Doom's Day at His right side.

'Therefore, Sir Lancelot du Lake,
For my love now I thee pray
My company thou aye forsake,
And to thy kingdom thou take thy way,
And keep thy realm from war and wrack,
And take a wife with her to play
And love well thy world's make.   (mate)
God give you joy together, I pray!

'Unto God I pray, Almighty King,
He give you together joy and bliss. . . .'

'Now, sweet madam, that would I not do. . . .
Unto God I give a hest to hold,   (promise)
The same destiny that you is dight   (ordained)
I will receive in some household
To please hereafter God Almight. . . .

'To please God all that I may
I shall hereafter do mine intent,
And ever for you specially pray. . . .
By Mary, mother, maid, and wife,
Till God us depart with death's dere   (blow)
To penance I yield me here as blive.   (quickly)

'All blive to penance I will me take
As I may find any hermite
That will me receive for God's sake
Me to clothe with black and white. . . .'
'Madam,' then said Lancelot du Lake,
'Kiss me and I shall wend astite.'   (at once)

'Nay,' said the Queen, 'that will I not.
Lancelot, think on that no more,
To abstain us we must have thought. . . .'

Out of this mediocre or even crude poetry Malory made this hauntingly beautiful passage:

Then Sir Lancelot was brought before her; then the Queen said to all the ladies: 'Through this same man and me hath all this war been wrought, and the death of the most noblest knights of the world; for through our love that we have loved together is my most noble lord slain. Therefore, Sir Lancelot, wit thou well I am set in such a plight to get my soul heal. And yet I trust, through God's grace and through His passion of His wounds wide that after my death I may have a sight of the blessed face of Christ Jesu, and on Doomsday to sit on His right side; for as sinful as ever I was are saints in heaven. . . . And I command thee on God's behalf, that thou forsake my company, and to thy kingdom look thou turn again, and keep well thy realm from war and wrack. . . . And therefore go thou to thy realm and there take thee a wife and live with her with joy and bliss. . . .' 'Now, my sweet madam,' said Sir Lancelot, 'would ye that I should turn again unto my country, and there to wed a lady? Nay, madam, wit you well that shall I never do. . . . But the self destiny that ye have taken you to, I will take me to, for the pleasure of Jesu, and ever for you I cast me specially to pray. . . . I assure you faithfully I will ever take me to penance and pray while my life lasteth, if that I may find any hermit, either gray or white, that will receive me. Wherefore, madam, I pray you to kiss me, and never no more.' 'Nay,' said the Queen, 'that shall I never do, but abstain you from such works.'

Thus the knight prisoner, by the alchemy of his ardour and his cadenced prose, transformed lead and silver into gold.

EPILOGUE

THUS concludes our attempt to make intelligible the literature of the Round Table as the product of historical events, prevailing ideologies, artistic currents, and individual talents. We have attempted in some instances the subtler and more subjective task of analysis and evaluation. We face finally the question: What was the general effect of this vast and fashionable literature on its own age and the age immediately succeeding?

Curiously enough, as a literature Arthurian romance seems to have had little influence in Wales, though it must have tended to keep alive the belief in Arthur's survival and return. It was rather in England and on the Continent that it made its powerful impact on history, ethics, manners, and on non-Arthurian literature. It was Geoffrey of Monmouth and his redactors and imitators who furnished the basis for English imperialism, for the claim of the British Crown to the overlordship of Scotland, and to some extent for the antagonism between the English and the French. The *Alliterative Morte Arthur* fed the flames of chauvinism during the Hundred Years' War. It was this aspect of Arthurian literature which Philippe de Mézières doubtless had in mind when, in the *Dream of the Old Pilgrim*, he urged his readers not to pore over the histories of King Arthur, but rather to take inspiration from the example of Godfrey de Bouillon, the hero of the First Crusade. For it was, in fact, the intermittent war between England and France which made a full-scale crusade of Christendom against encroaching Islam impossible. By one of history's bitter ironies, then, Geoffrey's pushing the conquests of Arthur into western Europe was a factor which made possible the advances of the Turk into eastern Europe.

Like all chivalric literature, Arthurian romance exalted the fighting man and feats of arms to an exaggerated degree and tended, accordingly, to depreciate brains and common sense. However, until the millennium arrives the use of force is inevitable, and the period from 500 to 1500 was not the millennium. So, it is one of the typical weaknesses of the Matter of Britain that the hero employs his superior strength in pointless tournaments and in exploits so fantastic as to bear no relation to the tasks and duties of real knighthood—in slaying dragons, battering copper automata to pieces, and unhorsing every knight who happened to be coming down the road from the opposite direction. It is this futility and unreality which Sir Dinadan derides in the *Prose Tristan*, and which in the nineteenth century the Spanish scholar Menéndez y Pelayo criticized: 'The motives directing the knights of the Round Table are in general arbitrary and futile; their activity is exercised, or rather consumed and wasted, among the chimaeras of a dream . . . they fight for the pleasure of fighting.' Direct imitation of the romances was responsible for the exhibitions of pomp and muscular prowess known as *Pas d'Armes* or *Table Ronde*, which flourished in the late Middle Ages in western Europe.

Nevertheless, we moderns cannot afford to be too censorious. We have our even more costly football matches and Olympic Games, and the athlete is still the hero of collegians of both sexes. Moreover, to the credit of the Arthurian knight let it be said that not all his feats of prowess were accomplished to fulfil a fantastic vow, to win the favour of a capricious mistress, or merely to add to the tally of emptied saddles. There were Saxon invaders to be kicked out or killed; besieged chatelaines to be rescued from the clutches of brutal suitors; traitors to be quelled; virgins to be saved from would-be ravishers; defenceless servants of the Church to be defended. These obligations, though often treated without realism, corresponded to actuality; and we find them formally recognized in Malory's version of the oath taken by the Order of the Round Table and quoted in the last chapter—to succour

ladies, to strengthen them in their rights, and to take no
battles in a wrongful quarrel.

That such knightly precepts and model heroes had an
influence on youth is suggested by the Italian poet, who wrote
in German, Tomasino de' Cerchiari (1215–16), for he urged
young men to look at the knights of the Round Table, how
they rivalled each other in prowess, but to avoid the evil
example of Kay, whose spirit, rather than that of Perceval,
was prevalent. In fact, the repeated contrasting of the crusty,
insulting, boastful seneschal with the courteous Gawain, which
we find in Chrétien and elsewhere, could not have been lost on
youthful readers. The speech of young Gawain in *Gawain and
the Green Knight* in undertaking the Beheading Test illustrates
beautifully how far the Arthurian romances had adopted the
ideal of modesty and consideration for others, and were passing
it on to the feudal aristocracy. In spite of the crudity and even
brutality of speech which one encounters occasionally in the
inferior romances, Camelot was considered, and not without
reason, as the best school of courtesy. Historical figures seem
to have patterned their lives consciously after the example of
one or more of Arthur's champions. The Constable Nun'
Alvares Pereira[1] chose Galahad as his model, and not only
displayed outstanding bravery in battle against the Moors, and
prohibited women and gambling in his camp; but also was
noted for his modesty of speech and demeanour.

What of the influence of the romances on sexual morals?
Arthur, Gawain, Guinglain, and Merlin were conceived out
of wedlock. Arthur himself was no 'blameless king'. Morgan le
Fay was a wanton. The most famous and popular love-stories
of the Middle Ages were the adulteries of Tristan and Isolt
and of Lancelot and Guenevere. It was possible for the
humanist Roger Ascham to denounce Malory's *Morte d'Arthur*
as finding its whole pleasure in slaughter and bold bawdry, 'in
which book those be accounted the noblest knights that do kill

---

[1] See W. J. Entwistle, *The Arthurian Legend in the Literatures of the Spanish
Penninsula* (London, 1925), p. 239.

the most men without any quarrel and commit foulest adulteries by subtlest shifts'.

To the second charge, as it applies, not only to Malory's work, but also to the whole cycle, three answers can be made. First, though the amours of Tristan and Lancelot were the most celebrated in the Middle Ages as they are today, they are by no means the most typical. It may come as a surprise to learn that the majority of the French and English verse-romances assume that marriage is the goal of lovers, just as in any Victorian novel. Secondly, adultery cannot be condemned too severely in a society where the typical marriage in the propertied classes was almost always determined by property or politics, and was often forced on the couple in childhood. Neither the *mariage de convenance* nor *amour courtois* can be regarded as an ideal solution of the problem of the sexes, but of the two the latter is more likely to be an honest and deep expression of feeling, and to that extent at least was more moral, though, on the other hand, it usually involved the constant practice of deceit. Thirdly, as we have seen, though many scenes in the Tristan and Lancelot romances are hardly above the level of vulgar intrigue, there is, too, an idealistic trend which reaches its climax in Gottfried's poem as an adumbration of Christian mysticism. In Eilhart even, and presumably in his source, Tristan's fidelity to Isolt is carried to the extreme of abstaining, though not indefinitely, from intercourse with his wife. Thomas adds the concept of life-long permanence to fidelity; and in some texts this permanence extends beyond the grave and is symbolized by the union of the rosebush and the vine which sprang from the tombs of the lovers.

Much of the idealism of the relations between Tristan and Isolt was transferred to the loves of Lancelot and Guenevere. Although burlesqued by Chrétien, it was taken very seriously in the *Prose Lancelot*. What is most astonishing is the recognition by the authors of the *Quest of the Holy Grail* and the *Vulgate Mort Artu* that such a love was a great and ennobling experience—even though it was a sin and catastrophic in its consequences. It may be fairly said that, in general, the standards of sexual morality in Arthurian literature, though varying enormously from one work to another, were higher than those of contemporary society. It is principally due to these romances that what we may call the 'romantic' conception of love, as something spontaneous, lasting, all-absorbing, ennobling, woman-honouring—though seldom realized in life —has long been and still is a dominant theme of literature. It was largely these same love-stories which raised the aristocratic woman from the inferior position imposed on her by society and the Church, and gave her at least the illusion and sometimes the reality of equality in love and marriage.

The artistic and technical effects of Arthurian literature on subsequent literature were, of course, great, but for the most part these forms and devices originated elsewhere. The octosyllabic couplet, the tail-rime stanza, the alliterative line, were bequests, not creations; while the soliloquy and other rhetorical figures were borrowed from the classical romances and from the Latin classics themselves.

Only the interlacing pattern of the cyclic romances, though not, of course, something new in the world since we find it in the *Iliad* and the *Odyssey*, seems to have been re-invented as a means of connecting into a unit the strands of separate *contes*. It was this type of patterning which seems to have been in Dante's mind when he referred in complimentary fashion to the 'ambages pulcerrimae Arturi regis'.

If one were asked to sum up in a few words both the greatness and the limitations of the literature of the Round Table, perhaps the best answer would be that it produced Don Quixote.

BIBLIOGRAPHY

General

A.L.M.A: *Arthurian Literature in the Middle Ages*, ed. Roger
S. Loomis (Oxford, 1959).

Bruce: J. D. Bruce, *The Evolution of Arthurian Romance from the
Beginnings to 1300* (Baltimore, Göttingen, 1923; reprinted New York,
1927).

Chapter 1

A.L.M.A., pp. 1–19. E. K. Chambers, *Arthur of Britain* (London,
1927), pp. 1–19, 234–40. For text of Nennius see F. Lot, *Nennius et
l'Historia Britonum* (Paris, 1934); E. Faral, *La Légende Arthurienne*,
III (Paris, 1929), pp. 4–62. On battle sites see K. H. Jackson in *Modern
Philology*, XLIII (1945), pp. 44–57. On *The Spoils of Annwn* see R. S.
Loomis, *Wales and the Arthurian Legend* (Cardiff, 1956), pp. 131–78. On
Celtic mythology see J. Hastings, *Encyclopaedia of Religion and Ethics*,
III (1913), pp. 281–93.

Chapter 2

A.L.M.A., pp. 31–43, 192–205. Translations of the *Mabinogion* by J.
Loth (Paris, 1913) and by Thomas Jones and Gwyn Jones (Everyman's
Library). On the Four Branches of the Mabinogi see W. J. Gruffydd,
Math Vab Mathonwy (Cardiff, 1928), and P. MacCana, *Branwen
Daughter of Llyr* (Cardiff, 1958).

Chapter 3

On transmission see A.L.M.A., pp. 52–63. Texts of Geoffrey of
Monmouth's *Historia*, ed. A. Griscom (New York, 1929) and E.
Faral, *op. cit.*, III, pp. 71–303; translation by S. Evans (Everyman's
Library). Text of *Vita Merlini*, Faral, *op. cit.*, III, pp. 307–52. Com-
mentary on all Geoffrey's work A.L.M.A., pp. 72–93; J. S. P. Tatlock,
The Legendary History of Britain (Berkeley and Los Angeles, 1950),
pp. 3–448; Faral, *op. cit.*, II, pp. 3–401. On Wace see A.L.M.A., pp.
94–103. Text of Wace ed. I. Arnold (Paris, 1938–40). Translation

(inaccurate) in *Arthurian Chronicles* by Wace and Layamon (Everyman's Library), pp. 1–114. Commentary on Wace in Tatlock, *op. cit.*, pp. 463–82. On Layamon see *A.L.M.A.*, pp. 104–11. Text of Layamon, ed. F. Madden (London, 1847). Translation in *Arthurian Chronicles* (Everyman's Library), pp. 117–264.

Chapter 4

A.L.M.A., pp. 157–91. For references to texts see *ibid.*, and add *Roman de Perceval*, ed. W. Roach (Paris, 1959). Translations of *Erec*, *Cligès*, *Lancelot*, and *Ivain* in *Arthurian Romances by Chrétien de Troyes*, by W. W. Comfort (Everyman's Library). Translation of *Perceval* into French by L. Foulet (Paris, n.d.), into English in R. S. and L. H. Loomis, *Medieval Romances* (New York, 1957), pp. 8–87. For commentary on Chrétien see J. Frappier, *Chrétien de Troyes, l'Homme et l'Œuvre* (Paris, 1957), and R. S. Loomis, *Arthurian Tradition and Chrétien de Troyes* (New York, 1949). On origin of the Grail legends see R. S. Loomis, *The Grail: from Celtic Myth to Christian Symbol* (Cardiff and New York, 1963), and for other theories Bruce, I, pp. 277–89, 342–62.

Chapter 5

A.L.M.A., pp. 218–50. Text of *Parzival* ed. E. Martin (Halle, 1900–3); K. Lachmann, 7th edn. (Berlin, 1952). Complete translation by H. M. Mustard and C. E. Passage (New York, 1961); selective translation by M. F. Richey (Oxford, 1935). Commentary by Richey, *Studies of Wolfram von Eschenbach* (Edinburgh, 1957), R. S. Loomis, *The Grail*, pp. 196–222, and H. O. Taylor, *The Medieval Mind* (New York), chap. xxv.

Chapter 6

A.L.M.A., pp. 122–56. Synopsis of Eilhart's *Tristrant* in G. Schoepperle, *Tristan and Isolt*, I, pp. 11–65. Text of Thomas ed. J. Bédier (Paris, 1902–5), by B. H. Wind (Leiden, 1950). Translations by R. S. Loomis (New York, 1951) and A. T. Hatto (London, 1960), pp. 301–53. Text of Béroul ed. A. Ewert (Oxford, 1939). Translation in M. Schlauch, *Medieval Narrative* (New York, 1928), pp. 131–50. Text of Gottfried ed. F. Ranke (Berlin, 1930). Translation by Hatto, *op. cit.*, and (abridged) J. L. Weston in R. S. and L. H. Loomis, *Medieval Romances*, pp. 87–232.

Chapter 7

A.L.M.A., pp. 295–318. Text ed. H. O. Sommer, *Vulgate Version of the Arthurian Romances*, III-VI (Washington, 1910–13). Synopsis in Bruce, II, pp. 324–79. Selected passages translated by L. A. Paton, *Sir Lancelot of the Lake* (London and New York, 1929). Text of *Queste del Saint Graal*, ed. A. Pauphilet (Paris, 1923); commentary by Pauphilet, *Etudes sur la Queste del Saint Graal* (Paris, 1921), by Gilson in *Romania*, LI (1925), pp. 321–47, and by R. S. Loomis, *The Grail*, pp. 165–95. Text of *Mort Artu*, ed. J. Frappier (Paris, 1936; small edition, 1954); commentary in *Etude sur la Mort le Roi Artu* (Paris, 1936).

Chapter 8

A.L.M.A., pp. 251–6, 287–90, 313–15. Text of Robert de Boron's *Joseph*, ed. W. A. Nitze, *Roman de l'Estoire dou Graal* (Paris, 1927). Text of Vulgate *Estoire del Saint Graal*, ed. Sommer, *Vulgate Version of the Arthurian Romances*, I (1909). Synopsis of Robert's *Joseph* and commentary in Bruce, I, pp. 230–43, 262–7. Synopsis of the Vulgate *Estoire* in Bruce, II, pp. 308–12. On Glastonbury and Grail see Bruce, I, pp. 262–7, R. S. Loomis, *The Grail*, pp. 249–70, and J. Armitage Robinson, *Two Glastonbury Legends* (Cambridge, 1926).

Chapter 9

A.L.M.A., pp. 20–30, 72–93, 256 f., 318–24. On early literature about Merlin see H. M. and N. K. Chadwick, *The Growth of Literature*, I (Cambridge, 1932), pp. 105–14, 123–32, 453–7. For texts of Geoffrey of Monmouth see references above for Chapter 3. For text of Vulgate *Merlin* see Sommer, *Vulgate Version of the Arthurian Romances*, II (1908); for summary see Bruce, II, pp. 312–24.

Chapter 10

A.L.M.A., pp. 481–519. For references to texts see *ibid.* For literary appraisal see G. Kane, *Middle English Literature* (London, 1951), pp. 24–80. On the Auchinleck ms. and 'Sir Thopas' see *Sources and Analogues of the Canterbury Tales*, ed. W. F. Bryan and G. Dempster (Chicago, 1941), pp. 486–559, and L. H. Loomis, *Adventures in the Middle Ages* (New York, 1962), pp. 131–49. On history of Wife of Bath's Tale see S. Eisner, *A Tale of Wonder* (B. Franklin, New York, 1958).

Chapter 11

A.L.M.A., pp. 520–40. Text of *Alliterative Morte Arthur* ed. E. Brock (London, 1898). Text of *Sir Gawain and the Green Knight*, ed. J. R. R. Tolkien and E. V. Gordon (Oxford, 1938). Commentary on the *Alliterative Morte Arthur* in Kane, *op. cit.*, pp. 69–73, and W. Matthews, *The Tragedy of Arthur* (Berkeley and Los Angeles, 1960).

Chapter 12

A.L.M.A., pp. 541–59. For text of Malory's *Works* and commentary see edition by E. Vinaver (Oxford, 1947). See also *Essays on Malory*, ed. J. A. W. Bennett (Oxford, 1963).

INDEX

BRITISH LITERATURE IN
NORTON PAPERBOUND EDITIONS

THE NORTON LIBRARY

Jane Austen *Persuasion* (N163)

Robert Browning *The Ring and the Book* (N433)

Anthony Burgess *A Clockwork Orange* (N224)
  Tremor of Intent (N416)

Fanny Burney *Evelina* (N294)

Joseph Conrad *The Arrow of Gold* (N458)
  Chance (N456)
  The Rescue (N457)

Maria Edgeworth *Castle Rackrent* (N288)

Henry Fielding *Joseph Andrews* (N274)

Mrs. Gaskell *Mary Barton* (N245)

Edmund Gosse *Father and Son* (N195)

Henry Mackenzie *The Man of Feeling* (N214)

Thomas Love Peacock *Nightmare Abbey* (N283)

Samuel Richardson *Pamela* (N166)

Anthony Trollope *The Last Chronicle of Barset* (N291)

NORTON CRITICAL EDITIONS

Jane Austen *Pride and Prejudice* (Donald Gray, ed.)

Emily Brontë *Wuthering Heights* (William M. Sale, Jr., ed.)

Joseph Conrad *Heart of Darkness* (Robert Kimbrough, ed.)
  Lord Jim (Thomas Moser, ed.)

Charles Dickens *Hard Times* (George Ford and Sylvère Monod, eds.)

John Donne *John Donne's Poetry* (A. L. Clements, ed.)

Thomas Hardy *Tess of the D'Urbervilles* (Scott Elledge, ed.)

John Henry Cardinal Newman *Apologia Pro Vita Sua* (David DeLaura, ed.)

William Shakespeare *Hamlet* (Cyrus Hoy, ed.)
  Henry IV, Part I (James L. Sanderson, ed.)

Jonathan Swift *Gulliver's Travels* (Robert A. Greenberg, ed.)

In the Norton Library

LITERATURE